# The True

# Teachings

# of

# Jesus

**From God Realization.**

What was Jesus really teaching?

Are you ready for the truth?

Did Jesus's secret teachings have anything to do with children and reincarnation? * How about death? It all did. Where did Moses fit into the picture? He was already gone. But his teachings were not and many people say they still follow them.

I need to say this now. Most people today are trying to find a savior that will protect them from pain and suffering. It can be a preacher, a medicine man, a great speaker, an alien, a healer, an angel but whatever one usually excepts means excepting lies as truth. It will relate to a programmed idea of happiness and what life is supposed to be. It will have no truth about a real God. It may temporary and take your pain away.

2

The truth that people know right now will change into something so different. The problem is it will not be the truth about the critical issues which will be changed into a programed idea of slavery or one world order? Who designed it? Seven billion people will never agree on any one thing never mind everything.

What did Jesus really bring to mankind? It was called Truth. It was the truth about Soul, Spirit and most important God. The real definition of trinity. It was not a religion. Man called it that.

Men were not ready for it then and still isn't. Man is creating the idea he is God. I call that the ego-god.

1.Why are children living in a world filled with so much depression and hate? Children are programmed within it to be what? It all has nothing to do with what Jesus ever taught.

Children are fed lie after lie. How many people know anything about Jesus, really? I do, so I decided to tell you the whole truth nothing but the truth so help me GOD. God, my body is in your hands through all the things good or bad I do. I only pray that I deserve that.

God is still teaching higher aware souls in the higher realms, there are many worlds we can move into. First, we must let go of the attachments to this world. Which is the hardest step one will have to take if they decide to start a true mission to understand God.

They do not use the word God in court anymore. I guess men thinks his word is better. We are to accept everyone doesn't lie if asked not to.

This will be the most profound book you will ever read.

I promise if you read this whole book you will awaken more than you are right now or ever were. It will help you learn how to understand what you really are as soul and not just ego.

Written word

Let's go over a few things to get started.

I can disprove many things in the Bible, but I do feel there are a few important things in it that I should speak about.

The Bible, Emerald tablets, Samarian tablets, the Koran and other writings were written by man not God. If I say I was with God, would you believe me? There are a few people saying they spoke directly to God. They write books on it and people believe them. You know why? They tell people what they want to hear, not what they need to hear or need to know.

Why do you think many of Jesus' own followers help have Him killed in the end? So, why do people believe a story written by Paul? Was his vision real? The same as Mohammad's vision with Gabriel was it real?

Sitting Bull's last prophecy telling the two main warriors to surrender which they did. How do people know it wasn't an alien implanted idea? Like the book of Urantia. Is it a demon's idea of a new world?

A dead giveaway about our spiritual unfoldment, the fact that killing is being accepted or allowed in any way.

Many people will say there is no connection between Jesus and depression. The truth is there are many things that connect them and the way we live in this world. Many children are living in depression. One main reason is the secret fear of death. The opposite of what Jesus was teaching. How is that? Man keeping Jesus on the cross in Christianity and even in Santeria.

Intro

Greetings. I want to make a statement about myself before you start reading my truth this book. I have Dyslexia and Attention deficit disorder. I see many things at the same time. To me they all relate to each other. Which is how living on planet earth is for me.

I have become aware of most of my past lives which is why I call myself a Incarnitiate Realist. * I became aware of most of my past lives. Many were so different, being a different sex and including being a different race before I even came to planet earth. So, my thinking may not be like anyone you ever heard before. I think backwards and forwards but mostly I am in the present. I am part Native. Their speaking is almost impossible for other people to translate it.

I will try to do my best to make it so you can understand what I am trying to say to the best of my ability. You will be the one translating it into something you can understand and not what someone else thinks it means.

All through school I had a very hard time. I did not learn how to read until I was in third grade. Reading for me was by memorization. I cannot remember things like normal people can. I can always remember what a person looks like no matter how old they are but I cannot remember their name. The same as I could never remember a whole song.

I used to get punished for a year because I could not say the alphabet. I was not allowed to watch TV until I mastered it. It took over a full year. I did get beat many times because of it, by my father. Home life could have been better. I had a lot of time thinking about the world and was always dealing with things outside the norm for a child.

What would your idea of what a perfect world would be? Would you please think about that as you read the following pages? Think about if Jesus was here, what was He really was trying to teach? What did Buddha or any other spiritual leader, teacher or master teach? Was it all about earth or not?

The next thing which is easy to speak about is the invisible spirit world, because no one can prove you wrong.

There was only one time in the earth's history when peace prevailed. You could call it, the Golden age and the age of peace. It lasted for many years. It was stopped abruptly.

All other times the world was in turmoil but by different forces. It was the result of reverse reasons. The turmoil at the time of Noah's Ark, Sodom and Gomorra and many others that go further back in time. Is any of it good or bad? If so for who? Man being the problem.

God is what?

The first ideas people receive of God, are all the lies of man's ego. They believe many things that have no actual help for this world or even the next. Most people are not looking for anything other than the stories they are told about IT. * (IT) in my writing will always mean the True God. People who live with this false truth makes me so sad. Then all the lies about Jesus make me even sicker. I am speaking about man's created ideas of what and who they think the (little) Gods really are. Then add in what they want them to be. Now, most people do not know the difference between Soul, Mind and Spirit. Please they are all different. If you did not experience them you will not ever know. You can hear people say their truth, which is usually the opposite.

If you study what Buddha taught you will understand his awareness. He did not believe in one real God for he did not teach it. He did teach about one of the first steps to becoming aware. That is called the Bliss state. A state that should be only a resting place for soul on its journey back to the higher world or realm.

I hate to start with the mind being the most unimportant part of our thinking. That will go against many of the so-called teachings of all the teachers out there. Now, I will ask you, a teacher of what? What are you learning, mind games, mind programs, false ideas, false truths but mostly false Gods?

After a lifetime of spiritual searching and finding spiritual truth there are two important truths. The understanding of God's love and God. I was given the privilege to truly understand the difference and what they really mean.

What man searches all his life for is usually a lie even if one says it is love. The lie is exasperated by the many people that say they love you, then feed you false stories about Jesus and God.

They are saying we are all God. They are your mother, father, your brother, your sister, your minister, your Priest which are all responsible. Then you are affected by your friends and lastly Government and religious programming.

Starting in life

So, let's start at the beginning of life here. Does your life really start on earth? I want to give you a bit of info no one speaks about. Very few people even try to find out why, because of fear or ignorance that comes from the mass programming.

If you understand the word reincarnation, you will be able to understand much more of the truth. Most souls come to this planet to learn. But not what they think they are here to. Many people will never really understand what reincarnation really means. Many people have their experiences, but how real are they? Thinking daily life helps one understand spirit better, then even worse God.

People talk about daily life like they are learning so much from it. You will go through it no matter how much you are learning from it. No matter what you decide to do in it. Follow a religion or not, you will think you are learning something important.

The things you are really learning, like how to build a house or how to make love or how to bake a cake, are not the important things. Then you will learn how not to beat someone up. However, what most people want to learn is how to make money and keep it. They still have nothing to do with spirit. I will repeat this when a boxer goes into the ring both pray to God to beat the other up.

Here is the truth that very few souls ever learn. When soul is ready (if their Karma is right) they can wait for the right family to reincarnate into. They will be allowed to wait for the right family with the exact karma that they have when they come back here if they must. People with lots of karma will not be moving forwards much. That will have to be worked out, it cannot be just given away, or taken away.

Childhood

Let's start off with childhood. From the first time, soul, which we all are, enters the body, usually a (Baby right before birth). The child is already learning about earth and the good and bad energies that people have. Children are always open to energy, light and sound when born, they are living in the light. * Children born in a negative situation do not see or experience things in the same way. Their experience is already directing them in a separate way.

A child being born with very little karma, but enough to bring them here again, can be burnt up at birth or near it. That is usually when a child will go through something that is called Crib death. To this day still they have no reason why children just die (crib death).

I am not talking about souls of beings from other worlds that are reincarnating into this world for the first time. In that you can see that very early in a child in their strange and negative actions.

Most children are gifted compared to adults. They don't have programs in their brain telling them how things should be yet. Meaning all their actions come from love, God and spirit. Children can see the true inner worlds when they are young. They see many things that will slowly be taken away from them. They can see spirits and angels as well as demons. I'm not sure the adults can see the demons.

From the start parents are already trying to teach children dumb words, and then make them believe in fake things like the Easter Bunny. Why?

For me at six years old many things were going on. I was being visited by a being that was beautiful. She was green skinned and wore a silk or satin gown that was very clear with a green tint. I could see through it, seeing her greenish body. I can't say I saw any person in the physical world that was as beautiful as she was. I met with her for five years. I would meet with her at nighttime and she would take me to many different realms. Teaching me many different things. Nothing she taught me had to do with the physical world ever. I didn't learn who it was until I was twenty-eight years old.

At an early age

My whole childhood I was forced to go to church every Sunday. I listen to the Bible stories and didn't believe much about them.

The only thing I knew the name Jesus was real, in my feelings and thoughts. I considered Him like a brother. He would always be in the background of my thinking. I always knew He was there for help or to talk to.

For me, I was gifted to have a lot of help from the spirit world until I was about 11 ½. That was when my mother told me spirits are not real to stop talking to them.

I was baptized at fourteen. I realized at that time I had four questions. I asked my minister them but he couldn't answer. They were very important to me. At that time, I realized I no longer wanted to be Protestant. I don't want to go into detail, but I did start searching for truth. That truth meant God.

I did go into witchcraft for a few years and even created a covenant at sixteen. I learned about magic from the psychic world or Astral world. During that time, I went into stage magic and had been doing hypnosis for two years already.

There is a difference in stage magic and psychic magic. One is real and one is not. The one that you can see is of physical essence. The one that you cannot see is of spiritual essence.

After searching twelve religions, my search for God was at a standstill. I didn't see any way I would be able to learn any more information about God Itself. I was in my first marriage, which took a serious turn for the worse. My first wife gave herself an abortion. It drove me away.

At the age twenty-five, I got divorced and that lead me to my next wife. This precious woman brought me into a religion called Eckankar. I was in it for many years. I had my first out of body experience which became a way of life to me. It opened the doorway to the inner worlds. It was something other religions didn't offer.

I didn't agree with all the actual teachings which provoked me to look deeper.

During that time, I met with Jesus, who was working on a higher realm. He is not responsible for everybody's karma like they wish it to be. He is an incredible teacher on the plane where He dwells.

To think He would come back to planet Earth to save who? People with a big ego, without any truth? They killed Him the first time. Why would He want to try again? They made Him suffer more than anyone else and now what would they do?

That is man's sickness trying to forgive himself for what he is and what he has created.

When Jesus was alive, how is it many of His own followers were also responsible for helping to kill him? I know what Jesus was really teaching. But it is not in the Bible nor did many people even know what His secret teachings really were. If you read all the Gospels that are found, like Mary Magdalene, doubting Thomas and even Judas's manuscripts. You get much more understanding of who and what Jesus was. Discount them you would have to discount all the other gospels in the Bible as well.

Children learn to work with angels or listen to their parents

When children are very young they are working with many angels or guides* on various levels. They are working at levels most adults don't understand. Before a child can truly understand it, they are already taken out of the spiritual world and put into the adult world of delusion and mind control. Having nothing to do with any of Jesus teachings or spirits.

This is only the beginning of children's problems. When children are born into a perfect family everything is okay. How often is that going to happen?

Let's get a little hard core. What if there are problems in a family? In most families, there are. Abuse starts when parents create what their idea of life should be like for their child.

After a half of a century of watching man there is a sadness how they never wanted the truth. They are always looking for a dream. Is their main past time dreaming?

Ok, if there is drinking, in a family there is serious trouble. Smoking cigarettes is a problem. If there are sexual problems the child is now living in Hell*. The child now is understanding the earth in a man's way (programmed ego).

First the drinking problems. Husband, wife or worse both drink. It is putting the child in a space of fear, anxiety and feeling of disconnection. It also brings in negative energy. A child has no one to look up to. If a child is in tune with spirit like I was, it will be their only salvation. It will help them in some ways but not all.

One needs a real role model one that they can be with. For me it was my Grandfather. The only person I respected out of all the people around me. My father being the most evil out of them all.

Problems being a child

Ego is problematic, as in many programmed families. They are programming their children in many ways, all in the name of free will. That means one's father trying to make their child a football player if they were one or are still one. A doctor will try to force their child to be a doctor. Trying to keep the family tree stay the same. It is incredibly worse in other countries. If a child has a religious family they may even be forced into an arranged marriage.

If a child is from a poor family they will be pushed into the worst forms of work. I am talking about child prostitution, beggars and slaves. Yes, some countries don't even let families have any daughters unless they pay a high fine. Unfortunately, many female children are sold on the black market or killed.

Just being born female is a danger in many countries. It is not the same for a male. Children living in family that are cursing, fighting and with no morals can only bring more problems to them. That will shadow them as they grow older. All the while the parents spout they are religious. It's another programmed idea.

If a child has two mothers or two fathers instead of a mother and father (biological or not) it will limit their actual experience. They will have a different idea of life. The same as what nudists do to their children.

No man or woman truly understands the opposite sex totally. Never mind what really is going on inside one's mind. Consider the idea of freedom, which no child has, as if at a certain age you suddenly know everything. When does a child grow up, 14, 16 or 18? I know many adults that act 10.

Human Programming

Programming starts controlling a little person's truth. Mind is no different than a computer. I will relate everything I have experienced about this. No scientist will ever come out with the truth about God or Jesus. Nor will any spiritualist or religionist. Ask yourself why? I will ask you that many times. So many people believe they have the truth. The false idea of what Love is and what damage it can do. I will say check it out.

Many of the problems stem from love including abuse and killing. That combined with religion creates a bigger illusion to hide in.

The only thing changing in thousands of years for the worse is man's ego. It is reducing awareness about anything real. People are making themselves into gods. Thinking they understand what God is by all the programs that were and are feed into their minds.

What about an alien's souls that came into this world for the first time. They have had many lives as other races and now are in a human body. Their sub-consciousness has ideas about other ways of being. How easy do you think it will be for that soul to learn the ways of this world or except what man thinks is right. Which is usually morally wrong.

What truth can a child find about God, Jesus or even Buddha. There are written words of a few people claiming they have the truth. We have the written word of a person. Most will say an alien, angel or even a little god is giving them that information. If you look at the real world you will see where we are spiritually anytime.

Jesus and Mary Magdalene

The Idea of who Jesus was, was created by man, by what Jesus was supposed to have said. His true words will never be understood by many. People created simple ideas from what they heard because they were uneducated, primal people and farmers.

Woman were not excepted in the days of Jesus. That is because of the horrible way man treated them. If Jesus did not marry Mary and have a child they could have never understand Jesus other than being a healer.

The way He was with Mary Magdalene opened many people eyes. That being the first elevated level of love on this planet. It did not last long in other people's eyes the ones that were not there so they did not see it personally to understand it. Therefore, the attacks on Marry Magdalene started. Man had to start to understand human love.

Jesus did not come here just to be a healer. He came to bring the truth of soul.

Man's ideas that all souls are eternal or immortal, or even equal, really? Prove it to yourself. People think they are equal to God. If people only realized how many races are here in this plane of existence. That they are all much different, in eating, thinking and abilities. The way they have sex and even the way they relate to each other.

Now many children are being abducted, more than ever if you really want the truth. There are way too many. One just need to find how many children go missing in the state parks alone inside the US. How many homeless people just disappear. Where are they going and for what reason?

So, few children have opportunities to learn anything important. They will be handed a computer to play with as soon as they understand voice. They will be hearing about sex and war at every level. They will hear the words Gay, transvestites, cross dressers, lesbian, homo-sexually, bi-sexual and one word I created try-sexual. Meaning just what it sounds like try anything. Actions like auto-asphyxiation and a super high will start pulling them into many things man doesn't need to play with.

A child is supposed to understand everything? What, how not to be? How not to act? How not to live?

While we say, we are not prejudice we are now more than ever but just cannot admit it, not even to one's self. There are over three billion religionists that are against the new age ideas of spiritualism and freedom. Is our world any better than hell itself? We keep creating this world for our children to live in. Why?

Deciding what you really need

I am sure everything I am writing will bother you at some level, the truth always does. Unless you are living in dreamland and just don't care. If you are happy there stay there but don't ever come out. If you do you will be facing reality. A place where aliens*, demons and men who have great egos dwell.

How much is being taught to children? Anything about God and spirit? Any truth about it? How about getting children hooked on mind programming games? Then filling them with toxic food. Do you really think God agrees with any of that? Does your God?

I will keep asking you what you know or at least what you think you know about God? You must realize it has very little to do with anything about the truth of why you are here in the lower worlds and not able to get past the astral plane.

The most dangerous problems on this planet is child abuse, child sex and child programming.

I wonder why people never look at any schooling system and what they really are teaching children? It is a programmed idea of what history thinks is important but it is not spiritual. Nothing about God but all about learning how to create a job to make money. How to fit into a law that is wrong and a total lie. Truth taken out of a person's own awareness. Filled with lies. Jesus taught children many things but that is not mentioned anywhere.

Churches are telling everyone to believe in God and Jesus and everything will be alright. Really? Do they have a clue to what God's truth is in any form? World peace is an impossibility for this world and the amount of people in it. It cannot happen for a very long time. The world can change when every single person alive with-in it changes not before. When that happens, the entire world will be different.

The hundredth monkey is not the answer. Becoming a sixth dimensional being will not be the answer for earth either. If you try going to the twelfth dimension it still will not help.

I am not ready to explain love right now. We have many more things to go over. We are still dealing with children. A child dealing with any of the above problems may have a long life of depression and fear to deal with before they are eighteen.

Depression is a manmade word. How about we give it a real definition? When a person young or old, is searching for something, even though they don't know what that is. They never are happy in the longing for whatever they may never find. That is called God.

I can only write this book this way because of all my direct experience. If you know anything about me it is that I live my truth. I walk the line always under God and Its judgment, not what man thinks the truth is.


New age, dolphins and growth


In the new age world things like rebirthing came out. Now people are giving birth in the ocean with dolphins helping. This allows a child to learn things that they would have never learned. One is the child will be smarter and healthier. Second an ability to communicate with dolphins. While government is working on the opposite end of the spectrum, trying to train dolphins to kill people, really?

Government has always known information about dolphins but will never release all they know about them. They are killing about 10,000 a year in army training.

I had a few incredible experiences with dolphins myself. I am talking about one in a hundred million people will ever experience. I am sorry for linking many things together but that is how life works. If it stays within the truth to me it is important and all connected. All things move and grow together on earth. We each affect everything else within it

Let's talk about children becoming a little older. They are being pulled into sex, drinking, death sports, and drugs. Is that the best we can do for them? Once there were the boy scouts and the cub scouts. There were the girl scouts and the sea scouts. We had boy's clubs that did things for the children. Lucky children are not allowed in the bars.

When Jesus was alive children would run to Him wherever He was. They could see the light* and feel the energy from Him.

Men were not as open as woman always were. That alone told us who were close to Jesus then. I am not referring to His close followers.

When your child gets their first boyfriend or girlfriend did you even talk to them about that? Many expect schools to teach sex to their child. They still thinking sex is dirty or wrong.

Moses truth on that made him create six-hundred and thirteen laws on top of the Ten Commandments. They came out of his ego. He is the one that created much of man's reality that is excepted today.

I studied many different religions and out of all the religions I studied very few had any aspect of what God is or could even be. After twenty-five years of my life I found something that could get me closer to God and explain It with many different details and images I was looking for. It was much greater than any other path I studied or even read about.

Out of two-thiusand religions on this planet and I would say less than five of them really help you understand God better then what you already think you know. Yes, there are many more religions being created monthly.

Jesus vs. Spiritual people


Jesus did something no one else ever did. Yes, there were many so called spiritual people but I haven't seen any since living in Atlantis over two-hundred and fifty thousand years ago. You might not believe me, but ninety-five percent of all history is exaggerated and out of time sequence and twisted into beliefs.

Carbon dating is not giving us correct information. To show you how wrong it is as actual proof, they have skeletons of dinosaurs with a human. They have artifacts of things which are completely out of place and time, which also proves the idea of the timeframe that the United States and the world uses is wrong. The thinking that they know when Jesus was here and what day he died is ridiculous.

Do you know science is so desperate they must relate to the Mayan calendar?

Without ever thinking who created it. It could not have not been human and it wasn't. To this day they say the Mayan people are spiritual. They were mass killers, every bit as much as the white man. The white man help killed 50 million of Native people in 500 years.

Jesus never said one word allowing killing. Not even in the defense of His own body. Jesus spent His short life promoting compassion, love and truth. Truth being the most important.

Role models

Back to the subject of children starting to grow up. Do children have any role models that are helpful in the development of their own mind? I'm not talking about Batman or Superman. I am also not talking about a football player, a baseball player. I would only recommend one or two presidents and even at that, there were many things around them that were dark. I don't believe sports make the world better. People being programmed to believe that following a role model will make you a better person. Well it could if you could find a pure role model.

Schooling

In the school system what do the children learn? The ABCs, one plus one is two? But what does God and spirit equal? So, what is next in school sports, football, basketball, wrestling, volleyball and weightlifting. They will never hear anything spiritual, religious, or anything important that children should know.

In schools, children are under stress, this creates a rippling effect spreading from child to child. Unchecked this leads to dysfunctional state.

There are problems from people coming out of families that are not complete. Children not having a mother or father, or not even having enough money will have serious problems. How much balance do you think you can bring into a situation without any spiritual connection? It's based on man's ego and false truth. It doesn't really leave much for a family. Unless you call the little lies important.

I worked in a high school in Toledo. The Native school was full. They had all the overflow Native children in one class together in the school I worked. Their excuse was that they were slow learners. Doesn't that sound prejudice at every level?

If you get the drift of what I'm saying you see a crumbling of a society before it even starts to get better. Sure, the rich go to college and get more programs to put in their brain. It has nothing to do with God or spirit.

They will be ingrained to make as much money as possible. Putting children in a place of thinking about a job they want that would give them lots of money instead of helping people or the world. How many jobs offer to give back to the people? There are many important jobs- but they don't pay lots of money. Medicine is about keeping a sickness alive not ending it.

There is very little about schools that teach children anything about family life, relationships, and even real friendship. People create friendships in school around the partying, bullying and harassment, that they all get at some time or another. Even worse is the sex abuse happening from all of that.

People say they are doing things about it. The school systems are doing very little. It is all a lie.

With guns in school, children are even more afraid. In high school comes drinking and drugs along with partying. It becomes the most prominent issue for the students. There is no effective way for spiritual truth to touch these children. There is no inlet for it to come into the schools. What little we had was already taken out.

## Racial and Gay issues

The next thing I want to talk about is the racial and gay issue. No matter what people say ninety-five percent of people are prejudice about something.

I think drinking should be illegal. Marijuana should be legal. The amount of deaths and serious accidents in the United States alone due to drinking is the highest of our problems. Now if you want the truth suicide is moving into second place. The amount of rapes and abuse comes from drinkers not smokers.

While the bad are few. Smoking weed is not a violent drug. It also heals the body in many ways. If you're not aware, the government doesn't want to heal the worlds sickness. They just want to make money from it. The prison systems are there to make money as well. They must keep them filled because of all the money they make.

The laws

Young people in high school and college are dealing with sex more than ever now. Many are being pushed into it while drinking along with all the sick minds of date rape drugs. I know how bad it is it by my own personal experience.

When a young person leaves school. They now must face the real-world meaning work. That starts a whole new chapter in one's life. They must deal with people that are so different and are only there to make money.

When a young person goes out to face the world, they reflect on their programmed ideas from childhood and all the things that happened during that time. Now, trying to prepare themselves for what they will be facing when they go out to work.

Nothing in our life style here in the U.S. has anything to do with spiritualism. Not our clothes, not our shoes, not our hair styles, not our furniture, not our houses not our cars or even our planes.

Pyramids were not spiritual, they were built to the deities. They are the closest man has ever gotten to God at that time.

There is a fine line between inter-dimensional beings, aliens and deities. If you want the truth angels and demons are the same. What your perception of them decides whether they are good or bad. Most angels fell and came down from a higher level. It is a serious thing going on and is destroying the human consciousness.

If one decides to live in hell to help people, does that make them spiritual? I don't believe so. It is the Bodhisattva question.

If sexual abuse in any form is part of a child's rearing, it may become a serious point for them when they must go out and work in the real world. It is the number one reason people start believing they need to be gay and never really admit it. In the real world, they must deal with strangers and other people they have no trust in.

Where is a young adult going to find spiritual truth? They start going to the seminars around the United States or the world. They are listening to all the storytellers preaching stories. Yes, they may be gifted with remarkable stories but I can assure you that's all they are.

Every young adult is usually pushed through a religion, that will be the only source one has. They will even be pulled away from that by their peers. I personally can't see many places for anybody to find the truth. I'm talking about the truth of God and spirit, not money. My truth comes from direct experience.

Children and young adults are already influenced to the max about relationships. The idea of having children is pushed on many people through their family or religion. If a young adult gives up their religion because of people around them, there is no spiritual steppingstone for them to take. Unless they are truly deciding to look inside themselves.

You can turn on a TV and listen to all the preachers talking about God and Jesus. Like they have a clue to what Jesus taught, what Jesus was about or what was Jesus' real reason for doing what he did.

Most religions take parts of the Bible to create their idea of truth. That has nothing to do with any of Jesus' real teachings which were the secret teachings and they are not in the Bible. Neither are any of the things Jesus really did.

Jesus married Mary Magdalene. They had a daughter. Jesus never saw his daughter while he was in His physical body.

The only way He could teach His disciples about love was by example. How can you explain something that is intangible? You can describe an apple and somebody could even draw it yet they have no clue what it really tastes like or how it will react in the body. All people have a different idea or their limited truth. Meaning if an apple is sweet, sour or bitter it is up to each person eating it.

The idea of teaching love is impossible if one cannot experience it. They will never know it. Many people never experience it truly in the physical world.

They have a relationship. Yes, they have children. They feel they're in love with each other for a while. That alone is not the total truth. They are not willing to give all the things into the relationship that will make love real. The most important is being able to give a hundred percent while at the same time starting to understand God.

All the programmed ideas of what love is, is now facing young adults. It makes them think how important love is. Men teach their male child that a boy doesn't get locked into a relationship or shouldn't. He's told to have as many girlfriends as possible. Sow your seed!

Most adults try to stop children or young adults from creating a solid relationship. The more you split something the less value it has. Relationships usually don't get better even if they began with Love.

Abuse comes in when parents force their child to move so they can't be in a relationship. Some become slaves inside their own house, which puts a child in many more serious problems as they get older. That kind of prison only creates rebellion sooner or later. If it happens sooner they will be in a serious position with their father and mother.

Most women give in to the father because they are afraid they will be abused. The abuse of children usually comes from the father and is allowed by the mother. I am not saying mothers don't create abuse because in my life my mother stopped me from having important relationships.

If that's not sick, I don't know what is. If the mother is sick, knowing the father or boyfriend is sexually abusing the child and does nothing about it. The boyfriend is replacing their husband and she doesn't want to lose her new boyfriend.

I learned that most sexual abuse is usually committed by a person they know; a family member or family friend more than it is a stranger.

I can look back to all the abuse that occurred in my life and I would say 85% came from family and friends.

One serious thing that happened to me and a young girl was when I was around six or seven. A stranger came into our house. It was a six-family house and I was going into the basement with the girl from downstairs to get our bikes. When a man grabbed us in the dark tried to make us have sex. We had no clue at that time what sex was.

Some things had to do with people I was playing with. It was an army game of hide and seek. I was tied up. I don't want to go into all the details right now. Not that I don't remember it all, 58 years later. I was a boy and it must be ten times harder for a girl.

If you go to a group of people that had similar experiences, it really can help you. When children feel victimized, they feel as if they are the only one. It is hard for them to understand. A child usually keeps it in and then starts growing with that pain, starts creating sickness of body and mind. A good analogy would be that of a woman raped, ending up going through the same thing.

If a person needs counseling they may try going to a group post on line. They will find they cannot connect to spiritual truth or God.

Psychologists or psychiatrists are locked into ideas that exclude anything spiritual or true. They cannot admit to demons, aliens or even angels. You can't say you talk to God. You will be considered automatically crazy. The system is deciding who is crazy based on a few sick people's agenda, not on spiritual ideas.

If you're on a spiritual path and you want help, I really hate to say this, don't look outside of yourself. All the answers that you need are inside you. You do have to rip down the walls to get to them. Those walls created by society and family members. You may need help to understand about how to go about doing that. That help is out there. Even at that you still must one must be careful because this is a man's world without truth and God.


Respect laws


I am a man, I seriously don't respect men. I don't relate to them, never mind them all being equal. If one doesn't respect God and spirit why would I respect them? All man's laws are man-made and have very little connection to spiritual laws or God's laws.

In this world, right now there are a few souls that have a clue to what God's truth is, or even what God thinks. Man creates laws and convinces everybody that it is right. If you look at the world in detail, you will see it's a complete lie. The world has very little to do with love or compassion.

As we move through this world we are pushed and pulled by man-made ideas of what man wants God to be. Even now with the New Age movement, the creation of false ideas like we are God and that we are all one with God. How can you be one with something you don't know? Are you one with a banana? Are you one with a monkey? You might say you are. Are you one with a dragon? Are you one with an angel? To say you are one with God, that means what?

Does that mean you can create anything you want including multiple worlds, multiple beings, multiple animals? That you can morph into anything you want? You can move mountains and put them wherever you want? You can turn a lake into an ocean? That would prove it.

You cannot do whatever you want and abuse whoever you want along the way without creating karma. You are helping ego to grow.

Being God must be fun and exciting if you are living as a God. What does God do? Send unconditional love to everyone? You may think so, try and prove that.

Please do this.

Please get out a pencil and a piece of paper. On the top of that paper on the left side write God is. On the other side God is not. Now write all the things you think God is on the left and all the things God is not on the right.

You cannot say God is all things. You need to list them. Please, I don't think you will have that many on the list unless you are naming all the animals on the planet. You can just say animals. You don't have the name things individually like all the different fruits and trees.  All the different flowers. After that, yes name the sun, the moon sky, the ocean, the further you can go, great. You can write alien races. You don't have to name all you know. I have a few questions for you to ask yourself when doing this.

On a separate piece of paper ……. put down God's feelings. Do you think God gets angry? You think God is happy? You think God really cares about what you think? Do you think God should? Man's ego creates a God of its own liking. If man doesn't like his idea of God then he will recreate a different one.

God is many things. The idea is to understand what God is at each level of awareness you have reached.

Buddha spoke to two levels the ultimate and the relative. God moves one into the higher realms or worlds of God. when one understanding of IT is complete.

The idea that this is the illusion was Buddha's idea. I call it the physical plane mixed with the astral plane which is only a limited awareness. That awareness has very little understanding of a real God. That means old laws of God that exists are just that.

Do unto others as you would want them to do unto you. What you give out just might not be what you get back. If you stop giving it makes you like everyone else.

In the third world things completely change. When you reach that level of soul awareness, one is now working to become truly self-realized. The first step before becoming God realized.

God realization does not mean you become God. It does not mean you can do anything God can do. It does mean you understand how you really are connected to God, and what that truly is. By that I mean, what IT allows you to do.

In every plane or realm that you move into, you will have greater responsibilities as well as more abilities to do them. The idea of saving humans will no longer be your goal, you will realize the impossibility of that.

If God wanted everybody to be a certain thing, guess what? We would all be that. You're limited ideas of God creates the world we live in and stay in.

One good thing is being willing to let go of all the programs and lies. If you can see the Earth for what it truly is I would compare it to kindergarten and the astral plane as first grade. Jesus said in his father's mansion, there are many rooms and you're not even in the mansion yet.

Following any of these religions, such as the Hasidic Jewish religion, Muslims, and Christianity, do you think you'll ever find any truth about a real God? You will keep finding more and more lies to follow. The same as the mind is being feed more and more programs to keep you from letting go of the physical world. Keeping you attached to the idea you think you know what love is.

What is love? Is it buying a steak and feeding it to your cat? Just sitting back and watching the news while millions of people are dying every month in Africa staving. Is that love?

Man was brought to planet earth for a reason. There were nine races brought here. There are only four races here in a physical reality now. The physical body is here and now. Yes, soon we will be having more alien visitors coming here.

If you look at some of the old gods like Krishna, Shiva, Kali, Durga, Bram and Cal Bram, even Jehovah. You will see God's of many colors and many are not very human looking. Many are exaggerated. There are God's with wings multiple heads, multiple arms and legs, half human and half animal which are still recognized. Lastly there are also the alien God's. They are all based on human's definition of God such as having super powers.

If you studied at all you would see sex was a big part of every God or alien agenda even with the giants that were here in the beginning. People call that working with DNA.

Think about how many people say they had a direct experience with God or gods and tell a story as if it was real. Meaning real to the world. If it was real to the world it would affect us. Unfortunately, what people are saying is not helping mankind move forward in any spiritual way.

Trains, planes, submarines, spaceships have nothing to do with spiritual truth or the spiritual laws. They give no definition to what God really is. I find it hard every day seeing the way people are looking at life.

The programmed idea of God is that it is all loving and all compassionate. What do you think that means to People, animals and plants? How about to soul itself? How do you think it affects the spiritual worlds?

I am talking about planet Earth I call it the hell realm.

Some religionists believe crazy things like they will have many virgins in heaven. Guess you must be a man. This means ignorance and perverted egos will never allow a soul to see God or understand IT. When the day comes that man decides to let go of ego, the part of themselves that is stopping their spiritual growth. They may then start their spiritual journey. Ego affects men much more than it does women.

Women are still in a controlled abusive state. In other countries, it is incredibly worse. The idea of being free only means stepping out of the physical body and you recognize yourself as soul. It will never be real before that. Yes, women are in touch with the compassionate side of themselves much more than men are at any level.

Another controversial issue right now, is the homosexual ideas being programmed in every person's consciousness.

KARMA and Homosexual Behavior.

I mentioned at the beginning of the book, about a soul coming into a child that had already lived many other past lives here. Many souls change sex in the bodies they use while they are here. Back and forth from male to female, soul will usually stay with one more then another sex over lifetimes. You will have been both. Soul steps into a child in this lifetime based on soul's karma of its past life. There are very few exceptions to that rule.

The family that you will be with and the conditions they are living in is equal to the karma you deserve.

I am sure many people will disagree, but it is very easy to prove it to yourself. Many scientists relate everything to DNA, really? Do you smoke because your grandfather did? If there were no cigarettes here, would you be smoking? It's the same as drinking. In a world of 7.4 billion people and 94% of them are poor, homeless, starving and sick, how can you blame that on DNA? They are separate and everything you experience is due to karma, not the body you chose. All people relate to the same sickness differently.

Do you think anyone would want to come back into those conditions? Please be real to yourself about the answer. As people say they have chosen their parents, or have agreed to be abducted. If you like karma it is easy to perpetuate karma. People do not know themselves what actions pay back karma. They accept man made ideas about it. DNA is part of your karma.

It is not that if you raped a person you must get raped or if you killed someone you have to get killed. What if you killed a village of ten thousand people? Do you think getting killed ten thousand times will free you of that karma?

The worst karma is if you kill someone. Most other actions will only effect one person or a family. If you kill someone, that person's family is affected but also the families that they could have had and all the families that could have that will not come. That I call a chain reaction that affects the whole human race.

Jesus said there are things that cannot be forgiven. The Ten Commandments pin pointed them at some level. What does that mean to soul? You decide. Most souls reincarnate hundreds of times back to the physical world.

As a child is being programmed by its parents, if you have two mothers or two fathers or just one or even none, your spiritual growth will already be affected. If you were a female in your past life and now you are in a male body, and not spiritual aware (few are) you are now dealing with different feelings.

Why do you think God created male and female? There's different energy in both. It is not soul that has to decide whether its male and female because soul is neither. It is the mind that gets hung up in it. The astral body* holds onto it in a separate way.

Being in the astral body, you will choose an age that gives you the most ability there. Who would want to be a baby in the astral plane, or a person hundreds of pounds? Usually twenty-six to thirty-six is the average age. The soul has no knowledge of being human. The soul has spent hundreds of millions of years in the lower worlds or realms. That has nothing to do with the body that it moves around in.

I say the body is only the car for transportation of soul. Allowing it to move around in the lowest level that is called earth now. What kind of car do you want to drive around in? It is different for everyone. It is based on your programming.

In a higher state of awareness soul doesn't need anything. It doesn't eat food, need air or water, it doesn't need legs to walk on. Soul is an energy and light form. It is a light being in the lower worlds of

God. There are five worlds between here and God realization. That is debatable in some paths because after the fifth plane you even let go of the soul's body.

There is no sense talking about that as many souls will not get there in a very long time if ever. Not that many souls truly want to.

If you tell them sex doesn't exist in the third world they wouldn't want to go there either. The idea of going there is already being depleted. The things that keep man here on planet Earth are sex, drugs, cheap thrills, sports and art. They will not need any of them on the astral plane except art and music.

Jesus spoke about what is of earth can be forgiven but that of spirit cannot. If you are spiritually aware then you are aware of the spiritual laws you must live by. If they didn't exist here. I'm sure most people would create them.

Spiritual things cannot compare to physical things. Energy from the spiritual world cannot compare to energy from the physical world. They are not even close. The spiritual worlds are thousand times greater. To understand it, you need to experience it. Once you do, you will understand the difference. Nothing will be able to fulfill your new desires.

Returning to the topic of a soul entering a child's body, albeit a female or male body for the first time. It may have been ten lifetimes since the last incarnation. * you were a female now being male this is different for soul's awareness.

Something to keep in mind is that the soul has a different awareness then the mind does. The mind is only a computer storage for programs. There is always an interaction between mind and soul going on but mind doesn't allow soul to be what it wants to be.

Soul knows much more than mind does. Mind thinks it knows everything. The Truth is always within soul whether mind ever excepts it or not. If you could use soul's awareness all the time many things would be different. There comes a time when soul can control the mind in a much greater way.

A female child with two mothers learns everything that a woman should learn. Even things they shouldn't.

Love for two women is different than love of two men. Sexual acts are different. A homosexual man is accepted as being feminine for a man the way he walks, talks, and even hold his hands.

Women don't have the same signs as that. This is a created idea that becomes accepted as how a person with a certain sexuality is supposed to act.

A young girl who grows up without any understanding of men will not have any help to understand a real relationship with a young boy or man. The same as a young boy growing up with two mothers is not learning anything about becoming a man that will help him. He will be fed ideas of how a woman wants him to be.

If you remember the book called (The Call of the Wild), a wild animal will sooner or later want to return to the wild. It is ingrained in their soul. If there is any abuse it will change everything about one's idea of life and love.

A man is very much an animal when it comes to sex. living with two women deprives him of many things. No woman understands a man the same as no man truly understands a woman. Man's programmed thinking is convinced they know everything about a woman but it is a lie and vice versa for woman.

Unless a soul is aware and in harmony with being male and female in other lifetimes (which most don't know) it will never be in balance.

What can two men teach a young girl about women? The programmed ideas that they have. It is so unfair for child to be forced in a situation where they have twice as much of one energy coming in and none of another.

It is harder for a child with one parent. It is very hard but that parent could always find the right mate for themselves to help the teaching of a child. I'm not talking about the programming of the child.

When do parents learn how to teach their Children something spiritual? Never.

The fact is that very few parents on this planet have anything spiritual to teach the child. Yes, there are only a few here that spent their life searching for spiritual truth.

How many parents know anything about spiritual protection. How many parents can teach their child about soul? How many can teach anything good about death other than the false idea of heaven. I am sure they have no clue. I just did a show on protection in the physical and astral body. Does anyone understand how important that is? How far into everything we do and don't do it goes?

A child in a foster home that has no parents they have it the hardest out of everyone. Reaching in every direction to find any truth. No one without the experience can truly understand it.

There are the things that go unnoticed, like possession, abduction and mind control. They can come from distinct levels, meaning government, aliens and entities. How many adults believe in any of them? Yet many adults except the idea of Angels. Like they have a clue to decide what an angel is and why they would even be with a person? How would they know what spiritual truth is? what their programmed ideas? Very few angels spoke to people and if they did it was something important. How many people today say they talk to spirits?

People have this idea that they are important to God. Religions push that on people as well as your parents. The great speakers out there tell you how important you are. I will tell you this, you are important only to yourself.
It is you by your actions that decides what you will move into in your next life. It will decide what realm you will dwell on or if you must return as well.

What will you be doing while you are there? Most people will be coming back to planet earth starting this cycle over to learn all the things they didn't become aware of in the earlier lives. The cycle of reincarnation is a cycle for a lengthy period for most souls. A hundred lives are nothing to soul.


Truth and awareness

I have created a word "incarnitiate". It means being aware of your past lives, more than one of them. People say it's not important. That is like trying to become a doctor and saying going to college was useless. How stupid is that statement?

As the laws change so does our concepts of freedom and free will. You cannot do whatever you want in the lower worlds no matter what you think. Whatever your awareness is you will be playing with karma in the two lowest worlds. If you don't understand God you will never see God. If you don't believe in God you will never experience God. You will never learn the truth.

Spiritual means?

You will experience demons, entities and angels in the lower realms. Whether you want to or not. They each have their own jobs. They must watch over certain souls good or bad. The idea of angels is another man-made idea, that they are all spiritual. In the Bible, it says the angels fell from grace. Michael was one of the greatest warriors. Does that make him a spiritual being, or God realized? No, it does not. Every angel and demon must learn their own mission and the truth that it has for them. The mission gets created out of their own growth in awareness. God doesn't say you are going to be anything.

Out of the lack of awareness comes a lack of responsibility. You are not or cannot be to blame for something you don't know. Jesus said that. It doesn't give you all the clout thinking you can do what you want just because you say you are ignorant.

Everything in life is the same as in death, everything needs to be worked for.

Everything you do is based on your level of awareness.

While being in hell, makes it easier to work things out and grow spiritually. I guess I will have to go into what the word spiritual means. It is the most abused word next to love. Most of humanity are convinced they are spiritual.

People are talking about life after the visible world. If you move into the astral plane, you will see many different things. Thinking that you will see all your family that you have been with in the physical world there is a lie.

You can see many things in physical reality. That doesn't mean it will be there in the psychic reality of the astral plane. If you are in a physical body, the mind is in full control. Soul is secondary behind the mind. It is like a back-seat driver until one wakes up.

People create whatever they want whenever they feel they need to. The same as religion created the idea that Mary the mother of Jesus was very spiritual. She gave birth to a child. How spiritual is that? Any creature, animal can give birth.  Immaculate conception? That stays un-provable.

I say this and nobody else does, spirituality does not exist on planet Earth. If it did it would be a spiritual world not a killing world after Atlantis went down.

After the astral plane, spirituality becomes obvious. There is no longer pain and suffering, abuse, lying, cheating, hate, anger or even stealing. There is nothing to steal. There is nothing to lie about. Soul radiates light and energy. That is not my idea of people here.  Here people say they are the light, use a lot of energy, but again, let them prove it or even show it.

Auras are what surrounds soul's body as a light. It radiates difficult colors by the vibration of it. Spiritual beings only vibrate at the colors of blue, yellow and white.

The colors red, orange, green, are colors of energy, emotions and feelings. Souls that lack all of that are usually dark.

If you look at the soul's aura of a person that is of darkness it will have holes within it. Those holes allow more negative karma, to come into it.

Dreaming, drinking and drugs affect the aura. It boggles my mind when people say they vibrate so high. If you could see their aura no one needs to tell you whether they are spiritual or not. If you learn how to see auras which is easy, you will see their true colors. You must have heard the phrase "I see their true colors". What do you think that means if they're black, white, yellow or blue? It is the color of their aura that soul radiates. They can even be multiple colors. There are only four primary colors. Black and white are just shades of colors in the physical world. There are more colors in the higher realms.

If a person of high awareness is walking in a crowd of people their light flows over all the people within their range of awareness. To give you an example, one elderly woman I met a long time ago walked into a room that was filled with two-thousnad people and her light as she walked in the door flowed across the room to the other side. I only saw a few people in my life that had that kind of light. It doesn't matter what she believed in. She didn't have to say a word.

To this day I could still remember what she said and she was talking about a pendulum. However, the only balance time in a pendulum is when it straight down. For on the upswing to the right or to the left it is in motion. The same as in our lives very seldom do we ever touch that balance spot or stay there for and any length of time. When that lady walked passed me she said I love you to me.

Mind is like a computer that's turned on searching and searching. When you reach the pinnacle, you touch the core of your truth and you step into that space. You understand all things in the physical reality. Not like a scientist understands it, but how God gave it to us to learn from.

Back to a young adult starting to find a relationship, a girl with two mothers going out into the world. She's going to look for a girlfriend or boyfriend? The question then becomes, what will she be looking for? It will also depend on how active are her parents in her life.

People don't have to except their karma. There are so many physical ways to change it. Good or bad it is part of your life. It was not always that way.

Children with parents in different relationships at the same time have different energies going on around them. That is karma. A young person with a life filled with multiple situations is stressful, fearful, and can put one in a very depressed state.

Children very seldom understand why parents separate. If it was not an abusive situation, they cannot understand it. If it's an abusive situation it will tear away at the child's core truth.  It is easy to see why children run away from home. They just want to get away from the parents they will do drugs or even worse commit suicide.

Most people think they have a normal life even a partial family is better than compared to people living in complete poverty, homeless and foodless.

The more truth you have the more problems the family will have. Most people never get into that deep of awareness enough to make a difference.

Feelings and control

I wish to discuss the meaning of the words happy and funny. Do they equal happiness? How long does happiness last? If it is a temporary feeling or emotion it can disappear quite fast. How about the balance I talked about to be so happy in one moment and being able to lose that happiness within a second? Happiness is a created idea to make you feel good. It is only temporary. If one can truly hold on to that for the right reason one is very lucky in this world.

When one comes into a new awareness of an experience, being of spirit, soul, and God life completely changes.
A soul that is tune with spirit is in tune with the light. That sound flows from God through the lower realms to you and then back to God. When it comes through you it always keeps you aware and in tune with what IT allows you to be.

When you're in pain what are you thinking about? When you are happy what are you thinking of? When you are thinking about God how do you feel? It sure is not your body.

If it's a boy with two mothers watching them dress, putting makeup on affects the way they feel, think and act. The same as a girl with two fathers watching them parade around the house and the way they act. Parents think they have the right to do whatever they feel is right. That would be great if they had a clue to what that was never mind what God intended it to be.

Moses

Moses created six-hundred and thirteen laws that were put into the Bible. I will not list them but many of them deal with sex, nudity, prayer and what you eat. People could not and still cannot live by ten laws so why add anymore? Moses spoke about nudity being wrong for many reasons.

People say he created the story of Adam and Eve, but did he? Moses wrote a third of the old Testament of Bible. He was out promoting the idea if you do something wrong that goes against his laws whatever that is cut it off. It is reworded in the Bible by Jesus later. Even that is written by a different person and is twisted.

I will put my life on that whoever rewrote what Jesus was saying was lying. It makes it like Jesus agreed with Moses teachings. Which is so opposite the truth.

When somebody says your prejudiced, do they have that right? So many people are all trying to force their ideas on mankind. How man is supposed to eat and what. How man must dress, how man must act, how man must do things, what man should do, and the ways man can do it. They were twisted ideas of Moses not Jesus.

Drink but don't get drunk. Smoke but don't get high. Eat. But don't eat too much. Drink but don't drink too much. Enjoy the sun but not too long.

Who has the right to decide any of that, the same as who gives the rights to an adult to decide when a child becomes an adult and can get married or must. It is a man's world and just might always stay that way.

With all the woman's so-called rights. They are still fighting case after case of sexual abuse and rape. For me, rape is the worst crime on planet Earth and creates the most karma for the person doing it. Whereas killing a person puts a soul in a better place based on their karma. A rape victim lives their whole life with it. The karma is not just for the person doing it. It is an act – that is not forgivable in the Bible. Should it be forgivable for any reason?

For children, this is a very hard world to be in and being a girl makes it much harder. Something the Bible written by man doesn't understand.

Boys have it hard when they are young. For some strange reason men love the innocence and the power of a young soul. They try to tap into it, use it, and lastly like to abuse it. Not sure how it all started. Somewhere adults had every right to control a child and try to force them to become whatever they wanted them to be.

I wasn't allowed to do many things till I was 16, at that time, I quite school and went to work. I received my GHD two years later. My mother and father was already split up when I was twelve so my father wasn't there anymore to beat me. Yes, I had abuse from my family as well as friends and of course strangers. When you are innocent you will always be the victim. My view is based on my actual experiences, not what is on paper or what other people say.

If somebody doesn't experience something they have no right talking about it. Go to a group of people talking about abuse hopefully they all came out of it. They would not understand it if they didn't.

Parents do what they feel is right, not what they know is right. One would have to be spiritual to know the difference.

How many parents even know what that means? Jesus taught many things including how much we need to give back to this world and how much back to God.

Even going to the movies and it's R-rated or X-rated, what gives parents the right to take a child in? Morals have disappeared from humanity. Many people are creating their own. They are filled with the idea of freedom and free rights. Hopefully you all know that's only a dream in the physical body.

Parents allowing children to play corrupt computer games which are evil is amazing to me. No one is stopping that. The same as movies coming out that are more violent than the last. Do people understand seeing creates images in your mind when you're sleeping or dreaming. They start becoming parts of imaginary worlds which become part of your subconscious which affects your conscious mind in the physical.

When Jesus walked on this planet, children had little time to play in most families. They were forced to work as soon as they could walk.

Science looks at things from a non-spiritual viewpoint always. So how can they understand anything important about any situation. It can only be related to money, fame, publicity.

Is what you read in history important? It sure would be if it was real and one-hundred percent correct. As you know in Native history what the white man tells us is about seventy-five percent lies. Science gives us false truth and so many people believe it. History will always be proven wrong in time, every part of it.

Even with the vaccinations they still are creating many more viruses. People keep taking vaccinations even though they have three poisons in it. The same as drinking water does. What is man creating without spiritual truth? Nothing good.

History about dinosaurs and humans are lies and are not understood, to this day, at any level. Yes, there's theories coming out every day but are they even close to truth? I doubt it.

Jesus never focused on how much time one has left but how to create what will you be the future of your next life. You would have to learn about SOUL and what that means to mind and ego. I am not sure any so-called spiritual leaders ever did.

Now with the new age and UFO world the little truth we had will slowly be taken away and replaced with a new program.

One of the greatest minds on this planet was Einstein. His truth is being proven wrong at every level now. Then we have Tesla who proved everything he said. I am going to go off topic a little to say Tesla worked with an alien race when he created two-hundred inventions. Those inventions changed mankind forever. Not in an effective way. That was not his intentions though. It was to make it better for people that believed technology was the most important thing. It had nothing to do with spirituality or spiritual truth. It was for saving mankind and the planet. It opened the doorway to the bad part of the astral plane. There are three parts to it which is not going to help man find the truth here and now.

His inventions are slowly cutting into the astral plane and the dimensions of that reality. That will cause more and more problems in the next few years. It started over one-hundred years ago. I could go into the facts but that would be another book.

I was a female in the time Jesus was alive. I was with the most spiritual woman that I knew that ever walked this planet in any lifetime.  Her name was Mary Magdalene.

Jesus did not teach the oneness idea. He did not teach what man thinks is important now. He brought light to people that were ready for it, regardless of age.

Many races that came here just disappeared and some just left. Man has taken many stories and tried mixing them together to create a better story. Basic concepts of the Bible took a small truth and tried to make it into the most important truth to the world.

Jesus did not teach the same things to his followers as to the street people.

Earth lacked spiritual people. I only knew one. I will go into depth what spiritual means later. I hope while reading this book you start thinking a little harder about that. All the lies that were given to you as a child. All that keeps a child from becoming the greatest he or she could be.

The true history of planet Earth is important. One should want to know how humans really came here. Science will come out with more lies about that. When man excepts aliens are real it will be even worse.

All newer stories about the Annunaki are mostly lies. All of them are so far from the truth. One needs to remember all written history are mostly lies. Each story is based on one person's understanding no matter how limited that was including Moses.

We are talking about one man. Yes, the Jewish people followed him. Considering Moses was a controlling murdering person. With his ego bigger than the sun. What did he really help people to do? Become free to ransack another country? Be forced to listen to his man-made laws which I spoke about already. Humans cannot live by the first 10 laws which he did not write.

Back to when are children adults? Who decides when they become adults? Many young girls must become adults, being forced at the age eleven or twelve. I know many children that are really adults, where as I know many adults that are really children. Who can make that call?

Any parent thinking that they have the right to control anyone is the reason for the world being the way it is. Humans are so corrupted, twisted and completely out of balance because of man's ego. It allows themselves to think they have that power.

In a new relationship if a young person not given any real lessons on love or compassion they are not likely to find real love. Out of all relationships few people ever do. Even then they cannot keep it.

When a young person is labeled an adult suddenly they are supposed to be able to deal with life. It is assumed that when one turned eighteen or twenty-one, that one day makes a person become something different. The right to drink, the right to drive and to join the army. Then in the end the right to kill. Who decided the legal age to have sex and get married or the right to kill?

Countries have different laws on that and even how many girls you can have. The problems are they are man-made laws being forced on the young people. They usually do more harm because they are going against spiritual truth.

It is instinctual to go against physical laws in some way. The idea of getting away with something is exciting. I will tie that into karma and how one must pay it all back sooner or later or they just may never get to that point. It is too much fun creating it.

I will repeat this:

About childhood and becoming a young adult, how much truth is given to a person about spirit and God? Yes, there are over two point two billion Christians. There are close to that number of Muslims, which already is about a one third of the planet. Hinduism is growing as well.

We do have two-thousand more religions for people to get into. I would say most teach only three things. One there is a God, two you are one with God and three you are God. People that do not believe in God don't need a religion. They don't need laws ether.

The religions causing the most trouble in a so-called spiritual movement is the New Age religions. The ones that think they are one with God or they are God. Boy-oh-boy has ego grown so much that it locks soul out of the body so that it doesn't allow the body to do anything soul wants it to do. The mind has created a program that is based on lies and peoples programmed ideas.

I am sorry about the lies in the stories of the laws that are here. Not one of them relate to a real God or even the truth. People follow stories that have no reality in any spiritual way.

Relating to science as our future is ridiculous. All the stories of indigenous people are exceptional stories but man has no truth or proof of it. Writings are not proof.

One person's story is also not proof for other people. Of all the written words how many are even close to the truth? Technology and machines don't create spiritual truth.

There are only three truths, yours, mine and Gods. Yours being created by people. Mine by my experience and Gods by IT's experience.

Even your idea of angels (meaning anything from fallen angels or even entities) are wrong. If an angel came to you and said, "love is all that matters" would you believe it to be real?

Jesus was not here to preach about love as many people believe. You cannot teach something without perfect example. You cannot teach by trying to explain it. If you did not 'experience' it you have nothing to base anything on.

You might hear a few things over and over because I feel they are the most important things for you to hear and getting it past the mind is not easy.

Jesus showed love not just by healing people that doesn't equal love. Not just by talking about it. Until He was with Mary, He knew only His love of God. That allowed people to experience it.

I need you to understand what kind of relationship Jesus had with Mary Magdalene. She was the only one able to teach what Jesus taught after He was killed (Yes Crucified). She taught his closest followers. Even in the Bible it speaks about that briefly. The way she had to work with Peter. Mary was the most compassionate woman I ever met.

I did meet Mary the mother of Jesus, (in my past life) who to me was just a normal woman. Though she was a follower, she was not always present nor did she have the powers Mary M did.

Mary Magdalene was the bravest woman. She traveled around the country hiding as much as she could. I will talk about this again.

Nothing says what Jesus was really teaching, it sure was not just about loving they neighbor. For two reasons, one woman was never recognized the same as men. Two the word love is not even in The Ten Commandments. People creating the Bible needed to control people, and the truth would not allow that to happen.

Young people in a relationship are trying to make enough money to support themselves. Having children with no awareness of truth is crazy. It's like starting all over, with the beginning cycle of life on planet earth without developing any spiritual truth.

How is that?

It starts because of parents not having Spiritual awareness. The problem is from your mother and father not teaching you about soul.

Your Priest did not teach you, your Rabbi did not teach you anything about God. Lastly the ministers and preachers did not and they don't have a clue. If the story they tell is true the world would not be the way it is.

I am a Realist. Everything I do in life is based on my actual experiences in truth. Speakers might have started their awareness from books but they did not have truth come from it.

I repeat a few things to try to get it past the mind. So that soul can hear it. Truth doesn't come from many people either. I am not saying that there aren't people who can help you. There is but to understand how to take the next step, to put you in it and have it created for you, is impossible. You need to do that. That is learned by soul.

You hear the speakers at any lecture or so-called workshop trying to teach you what? How love and money are so important? They fill your mind saying you're a great person. You are important but you need to make money. They are two false ideas.

A carpenter doesn't need a child to help him nor does any trade. A school doesn't need a person that is not a teacher for what could they teach?

In school, there is nothing they give to a student that will help them in a relationship or understanding love. Home economics was usually for the woman. Let's teach a girl how to take care of a home. It also has nothing to do with finding spirituality.

After the age twenty-five and my second marriage, I realized there was only one direction I could go. I hope you can see that direction is called forward. Meaning, looking for the truth. The truth, the whole truth and nothing but the truth. (so, help me GOD).

Religions have very little truth. Even shamans and medicine people have very little as well. It's all about programming a person to believe they are important, needed and then watched over by God or spirit. If that was even closely related to truth do you think everyone would still be having accidents all the time?

Drugs, drinking and anger will stop spirit from working with you completely.

I call it earth- truth. The experiences in the physical world have nothing to do with the spiritual worlds. Nothing. Please hear me on that.

To think that eating a hot dog or hamburger, drinking Coca-Cola or Pepsi is going to change anything. If you put on paints or dress things won't change on a spiritual level. If you work as a bar tender versus a cook, do you think you'll learn much more. Thinking you bought a small car instead of a bigger car, you learn something spiritual? Not beating somebody up today makes you better person, Right? Yes, but did you learn what spirit wanted you to?

Everyone has spirit to work with but how many even know that? I never talk about the higher self like many speakers do. Soul is not the higher self, it is you and who you really are.

All earthly experiences are just that. After a whole life with all the experiences put together what did you learn about God? I can tell you little or nothing, about yourself well, hopefully you learned something about that.

Learning to not create karma is the most important thing. Most people are not even willing to truly understand that.

Many expect they can just give karma away. Meaning give it to Jesus or a healer or just send it back to God. Like God wants it? I want to go into that a little because of the misunderstanding of it in this world. When Jesus healed a person, He would tell them to live in truth the rest of their life. If one was not aware of God where do you think that would go? It would go nowhere!

As Jesus said there will be may greater than He. Yet no one stepped up to that plate. Why would they think He must come back? That did not happen yet.

Unless you think the Nordics are that. In the UFO world, they believe that.

First sickness and disease were created for a reason. Mankind is creating more diseases themselves out of ignorance.

When a person deals their own karma, they are dealing with what they created. How many times do you think you can do something over and over, no matter how wrong it is? Speeding on the highway, thinking you can get away with it, once a week, twice a week or every day? Having an extra drink and thinking you can get away with it? I'm not going to list all the criminal activities people think they can get away with.

Why does a sickness come into a person's life? The first thing a person should understand is everything in the physical world is just. Even though you might not understand the implications. Most people don't want to face what they did to create karma in the first place. To say past life awareness is not important is to lie to yourself.  If you do something that is wrong you cannot just fix it. You can in the physical but not in the spiritual world. That meaning anything beyond the Astral world.

What do you do when you get sick? You go to the doctor and if they find out it's incurable, then what? One starts looking for a healer. One with a great record. Healers claim to be many things, being able to control God, light, energy. They can only say words to people they must except it. They assume their minds will except it.

When you go to a healer. You are already in a vulnerable state of mind of giving your power over to someone else. That healer already knows that and will use it. No one has the power over anyone else unless one gives it over.

I am not talking about rape and murder the sickness of other people for their lack of awareness of truth. I'm talking about one's spiritual awareness and connection to source, meaning your God and life force. When one person thinks they become healed, they spread that word. It creates more energy for that healer to claim more power over others and the people that come to him.

A famous hypnotist I worked with when I was twelve said that Hitler could control a country through the power of suggestion. A form of hypnosis.

If one is charging money they really need to think. Is it just? Is it fair? My feelings are how much can you charge for truth? What if Jesus charged money? How many people do you think would have been healed?

Even at that Jesus was a person that did not take credit for anything. He was the only one close to God enough to understand and teach about the TRUE GOD. It wasn't about His ego. It wasn't about fame. Many times, He would say to the person by their own truth and belief they will be healed. If the greatest spiritual person to ever walk this planet didn't take credit for healings, what person now has the right to? An egotistical fool.

A person without morals programmed to believe they are all that. Thinking they are here to save the world. We all are here to save ourselves. Not anyone or everyone else.

Let's take on the other idea that people claim to speak to God. Seven point two billion people on planet Earth and God needs to talk to anyone about what? Too many people really believe they are that important?

The ego they have consuming everything around them is incredible. Many people make it through life with their ego bigger than God and think their life is great. On their dying bed or when they step out of their body what happens when they face all their true karma? Now what? Even at that point do you think God must meet them? That is why angels or a deity* becomes part of their world at that time.

It will be only for a brief time before one is in the place where they need to go. Usually getting ready to start all over, whether it be on planet Earth or the astral world. You might get to stay there up ten years max.

The astral plane doesn't deserve a long friendly conversation. It is not a place where you should set your goals to reach. It is the first real step in starting you're your journey to enlightenment. It should be reached while you are here and still in this body. It is just like leaving kindergarten to first grade. All souls that leave this world go to get their next assignment.

If you die within about five to ten years of someone else in your family dying, you may meet them there. Soul has a period before it reincarnates. That being usually five to ten years. If it is longer soul will move on to a different family when they are forced to reincarnate. The karma of the body that one will move into must be the right karma. Do remember you had many lives and many families before.

MIND

You would think soul would learn a lot in that period, except when Soul comes back into the body it is being re-programmed by humans again and loses the knowledge it just learned. It's there within soul but mind fights with soul constantly. If it did, the world would be incredible, people would be aware of so much more than where they are at now.

People that think their reincarnations are useless to remember, in time you will need to wake up and learn and understand all the things you already know.

It's easy to think whatever you want, telling someone over and over till they start to believe it. Close encounters, the death of the physical body, near death experiences will start one's understanding that will not fit with anything you were already programmed with in your consciousness. Those programs have nothing to do with soul's real journey in the next world. Experiences will start pushing those programs out.

I want to take a giant step in teaching the truth. This comes from complete awareness and experience. Yes, there are dreams, illusions, delusions, fantasies, and just old wishful thinking. That takes in creative thinking and a creative reality. It is real only to you and the world you think you live in.

I became aware of most of my past lives between the age of twenty-five and thirty. At that time, I started doing a few different spiritual exercises. They helped create and build my spiritual enfoldment.

I was learning to travel out of the body. I was translating my dreams and logging them. It is a good thing to do. That started my true studies.

I also spent twenty-six years studying with a medicine woman. At the same time, I was studying with a Varjra master.

I spent twenty years in a path called Eckankar. I have always had many journeys in the inner worlds with different deities and angels. I was always dealing with Jesus as if he was my brother.

I said before to all the people thinking angels are all good, they are not. They are mostly fallen angels.

The deities each have a certain agenda they teach. They each mastered what they know and teach. No angel or deity knows everything or are God. The same as you. They know what they know by what they experienced and could see by their own unfoldment. That allows them to teach what they know.

Good or bad, angels based on your viewpoint doesn't matter. All vibrate at a much higher vibration then humans do. That alone doesn't make them the most spiritual. They are not held to a body that is in human form.

Obviously, the deities are so much greater in size, energy and light. You cannot compare them to anything else. They do not travel from realm to realm for they are the rulers of a specific realm or world.

For all the women that read this the highest deity is in a female form. She dwells on the soul plane which is the last plane, the soul body* goes to. After the soul plane, soul takes on a new form, but it isn't anything like the soul body. Why? Because now you are much closure to God. The vibration is so high. The light* is so bright everything is burned up except beings in a higher form.

When people start talking about experiencing total freedom, freedom from what? Air, water breathing, death, how about living? That is when it truly starts for soul, not before.

God grants you the ability to create. You can create your own worlds and universes here only in dream state. You can add whatever you want in them. They become real when you become in charge of them.

Realize one thing, your awareness of soul, for a soul is always trying to get closer to God. It doesn't' want to be stuck in the lower worlds even though it helps force soul to move forward faster.

Once you pass the third world you are higher than all the beings in all the other lower realms. That is not ego it is reality. A reality that most people will not ever know in many lifetimes. There free will is a lock and chain to this world.

You can tell yourself anything you want. The only way you'll ever prove it to yourself is when you start traveling past the astral plane up to the soul plane. When you can stay there you can truly call that bliss. It is not the bliss state Buddha was referring to, which is on the mental plane or third world. The difference is the awareness of oneself one has.

There is a reason for my madness about this topic. I know many people are not ready to understand it. The reason is it so important to have an idea of It, Is so soul will have a place when it finally starts its true mission. Jesus only spoke about that to His closest followers. It will also help you with a way to start understanding what Jesus' was teaching.

I cannot tell you about Jesus' whole life. I was only near Him for a sort time - the most crucial time. Mary Magdalene was my closest friend. She was a goddess of her Temple, which I was too. I was her friend and because of that I was with Jesus the last days of his life in freedom.

Mary Magdalene was pregnant. Jesus did know that He was to leave her with the most important mission for mankind. That being, finishing His teaching with his closest followers.

She was teaching Jesus' disciples what they didn't understand when Jesus was teaching them.

There were a few disciples that were very close to Jesus. Judas and doubting Thomas. Jesus knew He had to choose one person that would do anything He asked of them. He knew most would not.

Jesus' closest followers all denied him when their life was in danger. I am not sure many people would have stood by their truth at that time either.

When placed in fear no one knows what they will do. It is easy to talk about it when it's not happening. You can say what you would wish you would do if something happened. When your life is suddenly different and in danger, everything you rely on is no longer there. Even in a moment Jesus doubted God. Pain changes everything, including how the brain functions.

They say thoughts are the same as reality. They can be. If you allow them to become that. If they are realistic. Then again, there are many things you cannot create.

You may dream of growing wings or turning into a Superman and fly but, your human. Does that change what soul is? No, it is stuck dealing with the body for one-hundred and twenty-five years max.

I have experienced something once in my life like that. At that time, I didn't know what to do and I panicked. It was when I was standing a foot and a half from a Bigfoot and I didn't have anything on my body. That meaning a camera, a staff, a knife, or even a flashlight.

The moon was full when I turned around
I could see it completely. The smell was
horrible. I started to move and in that
moment. The big foot picked up his leg
and stamped on a log. I heard a loud
crack. Then I decided to run back to the
truck screaming to the two people, who
were there. "Get out the cameras!" I
truly thought it was running after me. It
was not.

When Jesus told Judas, what he had to
do he had no choice. He had to turn in
Jesus. No one else could have done it or
would have.

People look at it from a human stand
point. Meaning Judas was a traitor. If you
were dying and told your son to pull the
plug you would expect your son to? Do
you think your son would do it if he knew
he would go to jail or be killed? Or hated
by the entire world?

If you weren't there you cannot talk
about it. I was. Even when they came to

take Jesus away. He told his disciples to let them. Jesus knew what was going to happen, all the way even to Him coming back. Which none of his followers truly believed or understood.

There comes a time in a disciple's unfoldment or student's unfoldment, when one becomes a master themselves. At that point, one figures out the next step. They will take. They should not be asking someone else what it is. Yes, you need to be dealing with spirit only.

What really happened when Judas realized the consequences of his actions? No matter what spiritual level one is at you may still have to do something that all people will look at as evil. While knowing at the highest level you were told to do so. After the act, you hold yourself accountable for destroying the most spiritual person that walked this planet. Judas never saw Jesus after He rose.

Doubting Thomas was one of the smartest disciples out of them all. He was already aware and had real questions to ask Jesus all the time. Which no other of the followers did.

When Jesus was killed the disciples believed everything they were going to do was over. They only looked at Jesus' teaching as an active thing while He was alive. They did not understand His teachings, so how could they understand what was supposed to happen after he died?

When Jesus was teaching, one must realize he was dealing with hard working farmers. There was not much understanding of real wisdom and knowledge or even a loving relationship.

Mary M *

Woman were not recognized at all until many years later. There were only a few famous women in history. Before the 1800's. Mary Magdalene was the most spiritual. They created many stories to try and take that away from her, in the Christian religions. Many still hold sick stories about her in their heads, including most Priests. They are the ones that created the twisted stories in the first place.

When Jesus showed affection to Mary the disciples started watching. Most of Jesus' disciples were married. It's funny how later the Priests were not allowed to get married. Only recently some are. People never questioned that?

When Jesus was teaching He was preaching to the poor people in public. When He went into the cities, He still had to used simple words they could understand. And he always spoke in parables. Many disciples still could not understand what the message was.

In the Bible it says, Jesus said: "Over and over, I tell you, but you still don't listen."

Do you think it would be any better today? Why? Has man grown so much? What do people want to see as proof? I am sure nothing. I don't see it anywhere. I see all the teachers, Masters and speakers telling stories that are false. Making up stories about God and Jesus to satisfy who? Could the word be ego?

Angels always makes one story sound good. The most important thing to man is a healing happening.

There are many statements about how Jesus reacted to the people He taught. If you were Jesus, a person of light, walking in a world where people were trying to put out your light could you keep walking the roads He did? What were many of His followers willing to do for Him? It was very limited except it was polite in those days to feed a guest.

Jesus traveled with very little other than His followers. When he started doing his miracles people started believing in Him. Many people needed to see something that could prove it in their mind. Jesus did not come here as a healer. I will say all that many times.

When Jesus was teaching he was limited to the words of that timeframe. Now would it be any different?  The same as today with all the new age words we don't have anybody understanding it any better.

Words are just words. As an Native American Elder said (words are just words until they add up to something). You can use thousand-dollar words and sound like you understand something but truly, on the whole planet will people ever know God?

You can get a Guru or spiritual teacher to tell you a remarkable story to bring you into lala land. That will not help you in the next world.

Meditation is only one way getting you to the doors you will have to go through. It will be the deities you must go past when you get there. That itself is not known by many.

In the Emerald tablets, they talk about things that will open your awareness if you listen and then look. It will explain were Jesus went to learn His psychic abilities.

When you get to the gateway to the next world you are by yourself. You are dealing with all your karma, no one else's. You will be placed where you deserve. Not where you wish you want to go or think you deserve to be. Don't worry you will only be there for 5-10 years and then you will be forced to reincarnate again. I repeat this for you truly need to understand it.

When you have learned everything you needed to, then you would be able to stay there. Now you can stay there long enough to see the rules of that plane you are in. They are different from here. The rules change at every level you reach. Simple you change your vibration to that level.

Every plane vibrates and has a sound. The sound* is very important as well as the color of the sky there. There is no darkness like there is here.

All the words after the astral plane will be so different than anything else you have experienced.

The door should open to you not by you. God's hand doesn't go out too many. Man's ego made it sound that way. Jesus did not say that it does. In simple words, He said in His father's realms there are many dimensions or realms. In the Bible, it says in His father's mansions there are many rooms. Again, He had to use words of His people's understanding. Which was not much. How many words existed then?

When Jesus was traveling to different cities he was teaching to the people where ever he went. Many were without religion. They were the ones Jesus wanted to teach. They were truly open.

He did not go into His secret teaching to any people in public. He would teach His disciples the secret teachings in private. We are talking about two-thousand years ago the secret teaching. They were not written down ever. So, think about how many people do you think would really know them?

He knew the next most important things were compassion and Love. He told many family stories to the people.

Jesus changed many things Moses taught. He took all the violence out of the teachings as well as the killing. People don't understand why love is not in the Ten Commandments. Honor and respect to man were the keywords to Moses' teachings. That did mean man being the one in power first. Except Moses law never fit. If people followed them I don't think there would be anyone left on this planet. His six-hundred and thirteen laws changed the Commandments into complete control.

Jesus and Atlantis

About Jesus, in all my lifetimes from Atlantis to now I did not meet anyone more spiritual. That word fit Him and only Him. All People were spiritual in Atlantis. You cannot compare Atlantis with the time Jesus was living in.

Atlantis was incredibly beautiful and all people were compassionate. It lasted thousands of years. It was horrible when alien races came and help destroyed it.

Atlantis was a time when all people had thirty-two psychic abilities. They could move many things with just their thoughts. It was the only time earth was in a balanced state. Even the weather was always just.

When Jesus was in a physical body the earth was in complete un-balance. Love was not a part of life. Food was not easy to come by. People worked ten times harder than they do now. The word freedom did not really exist. People that were let go had to find another city where they could live.

People were mostly slaves and farmers. They had to give much of their food to the king. Even in that time being a woman was ten times harder to survive. Woman were always taking the blame for man's ignorance.

Where ever Jesus went His energy hit the town before He got there. I can say I have not met one soul with 1/10 of His energy and light. I truly wish I could. I have been looking for most of my life now at every so-called spiritualist or healer.

The difference from every healer today and Jesus is that He did not have to use other people's energy. No one person here on this planet right now has it like that.

You must look much deeper. Do you know God? Do you understand God? People that say they love God – they love the God man created.

The God that is all loving and caring. The God that watches over you and protects you. The one that forgives anything you do. REALLY? People that follow the Bible don't even know it talks about what things that cannot be forgiven. To think going to confession is real?

I like to go over all the things that are not part of the truth first. The things man created to protect himself and his ego.

Why man thinks hell is somewhere else and not here. If you look at all the sports of man they are all violent. In past times, the fights were usually to the death. Even in the Mayans played games to have the right to be killed in sacrifice. They created many reasons to sacrifice children and woman to their Gods.

Back a step, as I started becoming more aware of my past lives I started seeing all the lies in all the stories that are being told. There is a little truth when it comes to God and spirit.

I've read the Bible many times from cover to cover.  I was going to become a born-again preacher. I was going to church six days a week. I am not sure why I even tried to become a preacher. It was partly from a failed relationship with a woman. When I found out you had to give exactly 40% of your money to the church I said God is not like that. It is that way if you follow a few different religions.

I was going through a divorce and was searching for God's help. I can say I found it every other way then the way I wanted. You could say I wanted the perfect relationship, to have children and a respectable job. I believed man's program was right for half of my life.

Only to find out it was all a lie. Thinking that is why I came here.

It was in my last few experiences being out of the body recalling my past lives when I found my true mission and why I came back here even after being with Jesus. We each need to find our true mission during our life. If one wants to stop the karma in this life one needs to finish what they have created and stop creating anymore.

Spiritual truth is the hardest to find and learn on this planet. This world is so programmed about what is right and what is not. It is easy to follow the pack. You may get your meals and have companionship in a pack but would it answer anything important if it came to the truth about God?

People will usually take the effortless way even if it means a little less. They want to get by with as little pain as they can.

I saw people during that time did not understand or even care about truth. The ones that did it care, wanted to touch Jesus.  Children could see who He was. Which is a gift some children have until it is taken away.

Jesus was going to poor towns. Like He said, "he who have no faith follow me". That was very important statement. The kind of people followed that followed Him, gave up their faith to do so.

You would think Jesus' followers were getting closer to Him every day. You can assume whatever you want. Some were not. I would say many moved further and further away.

The Christian churches give much energy to Mary the mother of Jesus.

Why?

If you have ever read the Bible, everything is happening in the time of

Jesus, Wherever Mary Magdalene walked, Mary mother of Jesus walked behind her, if she was present.

It was Mary M that held Jesus' truth and power of teaching. I said before She had to finish the teaching of His disciples, including Peter. He would have never met Jesus after Jesus was killed.

I will mention Melchizedek, the person that wrote about it was Paul also called Saul. I want to mention Merkabah's as well as Ezekiel. They are things taking away from the idea of who Jesus really was.

The same as the whole story of the Annunaki. The more and more stories I hear make me think the whole human race is being programmed in an extremely unhealthy way. They have accepted what Constantine and a few other people created, meaning their Bible. They handpicked what they wanted said and the way it was going to be given to the people.

A Goddess did whatever they wanted. They would never give their virginity to a man. That is the sick reasoning why the Hasidic Jewish people created a ceremony of a man that called in a Rabi to take the virginity of a girl away. Only then, a woman could get married. (She had to be a Virgin). That is the sick truth and alive today. You will hear lies about it. Why did every temple have a phallic symbol in them? It is not common knowledge that there is a crystal ball in many churches.

I mention all these things because I did work in many religious people's homes and in many temples and churches as well. I talk to many Priests, Rabbis, Ministers, Preachers and Medicine people. Listening to their stories and their truth, if they had any? I can only say their truth meaning it happened on earth but not as in it did in heaven.

All this time I was studying a path that taught about Soul Travel. I learned and studied for twenty years along with two other paths. One was Native teachings and one was the Vajra teachings.

While all that was taking place, I was working with three Deities.

As you read through this book I will capitalize things that deserve it. Man doesn't deserve that much respect. There are the little Gods and beings that have brought many things to this world.

The angels only bring warnings of disasters. They can bring light. They may take you into it.

I am sure you will have a challenging time excepting everything I am saying. I must stand before God and none other.

When people die they do not get the privilege of seeing God. It is not a gift of death of the physical. It is not just given to many souls. People stuck with their big (little) ego want to believe they are important. People want to tell you as well. The lies keep growing and so does the population.

I said I had over five near death experiences. Only one of them brought me directly to God. That happened in my life three times.

An angel or deity will take you to God, two times before you are allowed there by yourself one time. That is the God's truth. It will only be for a few seconds in our time. It will not be like you get a story. It would be more like turning on a light and off. Not who was holding it and how to use it.

All the answers you were looking for will be answered instantly. You will finally start your true mission in all Worlds or planes and you will now take you first real step into the spiritual worlds.

Your first battle will be going past the Gods of the astral plane. There are three there. Then one on every plane to the higher worlds. They are Jehovah, Brahma and Cal-Brahma. Yes, Moses' God. Lucifer* is there as well. I did not hear any story of a person or an alien speaking about a true God in any way. The programmed idea of what God is just a man's created idea. Coming from their ego.

Man, always made himself more important than a woman. Always creating the notion that whatever one man goes through all men will go through too. Ideas of forgiveness and what they say Jesus came here for was the biggest lie.

Two of the gospels were added to create man's story instead of Gods. Like all men can be forgiven. That all bad men go to a hell. Like all men need to be controlled and filled with a program. That program became a program of killing.

Hell- Why?

All men were already there on planet earth. (hell). It is not a place to go to, but to get out of. This is the only place souls can experience pain and see it in every form. We feel it at every level right up to death. This is one of the only places Love is a lie and being mutated into many horrible things. It leads many people into abuse, killing and even rape.

Man has and is still trying to remove any idea of a real God from people. They feed them the false truth that they are or even one with IT.

If man was truly one with God and we were all one here on this planet, I would command God to destroy my soul. I could not agree with God being ignorant like humanity is. If I did everything right I would say I don't belong here. I know God is not anything like man.

Please take out a piece of paper and a pen again. Write the qualities of GOD.

Then write the wrath of God. Put the two of them side by side.

After that start telling yourself what God like traits you have or think you have. You don't have any of the abilities God has. Wishful thinking will only last so long. In the end, you face all your lies and even your false truths.

There might be a few people on planet earth that are different. Never more than nine. Which is the most sacred number for many reason.

Three a major aspect of it. As the Christians say the Father, Son and Holy Ghost. The three parts of an atom. One other is the three states water, ice and a gas are all forms of the same thing. They are all the same substance. The most important God, soul and spirit.

I always knew that was the same with Magnetism, Gravity, and Energy.

They are the constituents for all things in the first five worlds of God. The last is where Soul makes it decision if it will ever move on or stay on the soul plane.

God allows you that when you are there. Only when you deserve to be there. You cannot get there any other way; no angel or deity has that power. It is now between you and God only.

You can stay and work with the Goddess of the fifth world. She takes form for the souls reaching that level.

The other Gods I call the little Gods are in a male form. They are in control of each world. There are many deities that are female form. It is what they chose to take in and be.

I am telling you my truth. I am telling you that everything I have given to you already, you can prove to yourself. If you really want the truth, not the truth you were programmed with.

While I am talking about part of unfoldment I wanted to talk about what you listen to.

The higher self is not higher. It is just you. You are over riding the ego. That is all. The ego is a part of the brain that tries to allow soul, your true self, to be aware of itself and the body it is using. That means you know right action at any given time if you listen. Mind always tries to stop it. The mind treats it as a virus and tries to block it. That is the same as a virus program in your computer. It is working backwards.

For your protection, I will give you two different things to help you in life.

One: How do you listen to soul?

Two: How to pray.

There is only one mission for your soul being in a body. You can choose to find it or not. You play the games or you don't. There are many things that seem important and can stay that way all your life. If certain things did not happen, many people would never move forward or try to.

If someone is on drugs and someone keeps supplying them, they might call it their own so-called bliss. When it suddenly stops they will start going crazy.

The five passions of the mind that keeps man happy and wanting to stay here is Lust, Greed, Anger, Vanity and Attachment. We have them all, they all need to be under your control.

In my viewpoint, the two that will keep you reincarnating is anger and attachment. Jesus taught many things and in His teaching, they are what stops one from understanding what He was really teaching. WHY?

Anger is something in the physical that allows you to create more and more Karma. When you get angry it completely disconnects your body from soul awareness. During that time, you are running on a computer program that is out of control. During that time, many terrible things happen. The same as when one gets drunk or high on heavy drugs. The worst things can happen. Soul can only watch. The mind thinks it is in full control.

The other emotion, attachment can be to anything. Things like family, sex, animals, cheap thrills- excitement. It can be to nature and even solid objects like cars. Coming back to get a better car. You might want to come back to see your children in your last life, thinking you could come back and make things better.

If your karma is still tied to that. Karma must be paid in full. I am not sure people understand what that really means. It is like owing on your car loan for five years and you just paid off your last car payment.

It is about people you let die, or people you hurt.

A man thinks he can go around taking a girl's virginity never mind repeatedly just because he can. The karma he is creating is incredible. If he lives his life like that I

would say he might not ever leave the
lower world for another one-hundred
lifetimes or more.

In some religions, they think they can
be forgiven. They should read their own
Bible. A person going to a healer, to heal a
sickness - which equals karma.
Unfortunately, that will only be temporary.

In Jesus' teachings to people that came
to Him, not His disciples what I call His
general teachings, they were about
understanding their mistakes and
changing them. If one acknowledges,
one's own actions and would repeat them,
what makes people think Jesus or God
would have to forgive them again?

If everyone learned by their mistakes
imagine all the people living from a perfect
place of truth, knowing about their own
actions.

Jesus said many things to His disciples.
He told them repeatedly saying "still you

don't listen". Jesus was giving them a new teaching. Many could not understand it.

Jesus would tell people that were healed, he said many times by their own faith they were healed. Jesus never had an ego. Never showed anything other than the truth of soul to His followers.

Jesus said many times to the people go out and purify your life and then you will now know the truth. He did not say come back when you forget it.

People in history created stories. I cannot say I was able to check them all out. No matter what people say about the time line, time travel and the many bodies you have. You have a set number of past lives you lived. You were not everything in all times and all places. No one is or was.

I became aware of most of my past lives. It is easy to relate it to time. You cannot be two people at the same time. You were not an army man killing your

Native body. You can twist the information and think that.

Why?

Realizing you killed someone and then trying to hide from it.

I went through many lives. I realized many things about my soul's journey. Out of them all only two were most important not including the present.

Atlantis was the only time in earth's History when the earth was in a balanced state. It was really the Garden of Eden. Everything was beautiful, peaceful, loving and people lived in complete compassion.

Without going into everything we did, we did not have to speak. One could not lie nor wanted to. They did not need to. People had the all the psychic ability of the astral plane.

Atlantis was destroyed by certain alien races and sunk.

Out of the nine races that were here, four stayed living on planet earth. The five others left this world. If you don't know the Black, Red, White and Yellow races. Five other races left. They each became spiritual beings, higher life forms. One of each race became a little God.

We are here to learn, not what everyone thinks. I could write a whole book on that alone.

Here are few simple ideas. You are nice to your dog or cat, right? Yet you will eat a cow, a lamb and even a baby calf. How's that? You, love one person and hate another. They are controlled by feelings. Feelings are mostly controlled and used by the mind. The senses that guide it are smell, taste, nerves, sight, feeling of touch, feelings of emotions, warmth and cold. Soul is not part of the mind even though many great spiritualists say it is.

Your brain is solid, your body is solid-yes 76 percent water. Soul is not a gas. It is something not of the physical world. The body goes back to the ground from which it came out of. The gift it had was being used by soul.

I want you to remember that when I say earth and the lower world I refer to the astral plane as well. They are very closely connected. When Soul leaves planet earth to go to the astral plane things appear the same and some things don't. You can do things some people might say making them God like. Your astral body doesn't have to eat. The astral body can walk as well as it can fly. It now has many of the true psychic abilities back again.

You don't have the ability to kill anyone. Age is decided by you. Soul is always aware of all its past lives but the mind is not. When your body dies soul is aware, without mind. It now must deal with karma. That will be the reason for it having to have to come back.

In the astral world soul picks an age usually twenty-five to thirty-five in most cases. It would not pick two years old or one-hundred. It would be in a lost state of awareness. You are not born into a family on the astral plane. You will be given a mission when you get there for as long as you are there. The astral plane is not the vacation spot. Dying is not just letting go of any form of ideas of work.

When soul realizes it has a mission it is that alone that allows one to move forward in one's mission at any level and it only gets better.

If you want to stay in the bliss state Buddha spoke about, then you lose everything you are, nothing (void of awareness of self) for a very long time.

I am not speaking about time like it is here even. In each world time becomes greater or lesser depending on how you look at it. A hundred and twenty-five years here (max) is like a thousand years there. That meaning how much you can do in that time. When in bliss you give up awareness for a long time. You are just vibrating in the light* and sound current.

When and if you learn about leaving the body you will be able to do many things in the half hour earth time which can seem like days there. Not that anything there is based on a rotation of something around something else. You also don't age. Even if you were a child when you died. Your astral body age will be based on many other lives you had.

People without any awareness will take an old body and stay in it for as long as they are forced to stay on the astral plane.

When you listen to the Native teaching you will hear their story. They spoke about the green pastures where the Elders are. They are stuck there from their programming. Which many so-called religionists do as well.

Planet earth age gives the idea of wisdom and knowledge. It can be good or it can be very bad.

On the astral plane, you will find the opposite of all the programs. Many souls are still trying to run on programs, like thinking your mother or grandmother must be old if you do meet them. That is another programmed idea. The astral plane is not a nursing school. It is not a senior citizen center either.

Each Soul is now responsible. If one learns that only do can they will get to stay there. Most will need to reincarnate to relearn their truth.

Jesus taught about how important good and bad karma is. With God, all things are karma-less. Without God, all things are tied to both.

How do you find the truth? There is only one way and people have a problem with that.

First step is breaking the ego down and then looking for the truth. The first step is very easy. It is spiritual meditation. Most meditation is not spiritual. It is a mind game. Even trying to stop mind from thinking is a mind game.

If you say not wanting to want, it is still wanting. You must understand the mind from a spiritual place and then a physical place.

Why we live here for the most part is people trying to learn how to live in world peace. Do you see peace growing anywhere? Life is not about peace.

The concept of love? Is the earth about love, love of a car, a house, money, your children and add yes, your mate? How long does it last, five to fifty years? Is it always getting better?

Love starts as a program from what you are told it is and what it isn't when you were little. All children of human incarnations have their own understanding at birth and that is always under attack from that time on.

Many alien races are incarnating to this planet now. They each have different views and a different awareness then a human reincarnating does.

If one seeks out true love, they will then start their true mission finding God. They will not be looking for another boyfriend or girlfriend. Although a relationship may be beneficial.

In Jesus' times meditation and ceremony was an evil act. People were put to death that were seen practicing it. That carried into the present to killing witches. Native people were called demons.

In case you do not understand killing, it is a person losing their life by someone else. We don't need more words to describe it. There are hundreds of ways so let's keep it simple.

To show Man's own ignorance, look at Moses coming off the mountain and having 3000 people killed. Then the British and Spanish coming into the US and killing fifty million Native people.

I am against guided meditations when one tries to bring a person to a certain place but not if it is only used to get one started. The idea they need to walk with you to make it happen is a lie. Your experience will always have something important whether you remember it or not. I am not speaking about just trying to relax the body. That will come out of it automatically.

The idea is to start understanding how soul leaves the body. That is the most important thing one needs to learn from birth to the present. A child is aware at many distinct levels and needs to learn how to sustain that.

Are you ready to look for the truth? Are you ready to give up all your lies? Please I am not forcing my truth on you. You might think so. I am getting you ready to face your own. People will always be fighting their programmed truth. Many will never get past it either.

A very severe problem is all the new age speakers creating so many false ideas. Beautiful ideas that exist only in dreamland or I call it lala land.

Something that might help you again, write down your ideas or thoughts, write them or you will forget them.

Right now, people are so desperate they have no time to search out truth and are looking for a super role model.

Have you ever wondered why all the comic books you've read, when you were little are now movies and many adults are going to them? The idea for a super figure to come out to save humanity and make it the dream (life) that many people think it should be.

To think that any religion, path or alien has any answers that will help man pull out of this most severe problem, we are or lost in, is the biggest lie.

If you are ready for knowledge about Jesus, I feel now is the time. This is a person that walked this world in a time when people had no truth about a real God or spiritual path. Spiritual meaning connecting to a real GOD, not a deity.

They thought a statue, picture, artifact would save them and protect them. Anything with super power had to be God and protecting them.

All the cults and psychic paths use other people's energy to make something happen. Jesus was one of a kind. He never used other people by saying he was super powered. He told many people to their face that it was their own truth. Really it was their awareness. Which many people in that time did not understand.

Jesus walked with nothing and asked for nothing. He gave of himself in every conceivable way.

He brought truth, not just love to this world. He told the poor people simple things. People with a religion were always around him looking to compare their truth with His. I learned myself the older and poorer people are more connected to compassion. The richer one is the further one is from it.

Jesus was traveling where ever He could to bring the truth. Do you really think people would be afraid of love even in those times? Truth is the same still to this day. People are afraid of true love.

What do you think Jesus' real mission was about? It was not anything like Moses teaching. He had secret meetings. Why? To speak about how great love is? How to make love work in a relationship? It doesn't even work today.

Now let's break to the time Jesus faced the darkness, devil or Lucifer which ever you prefer. It lasted forty days and forty nights. Who kept that record? Who told that story and why? Jesus did with His followers. It was important.

Why?

In Jesus' words, Why, did He speak about the walking dead and false prophets? He spoke about how people will be following everything except the truth. Truth being the most important concept then as it is now.

When He said, "go out and sin*no more", who was He talking to? Does any Christian even know what a sin is? Moses did not. It is called karma today. He helped create it. How many children and people died from Moses truth?

Jesus said you are not accountable for what you don't know and you are for what you do know. How much did Moses really know? I would say very little about man, even less about woman and children and nothing about God.

In his own way Moses spawned a religion that was sick in its creation. Our country called the U.S. is only walking in the evil footprints that he created.

Who is the Government afraid of the most today? Why would it be the Native people? They were called the demons. Why in all the events of our history, the fear just grew out of the darkness, that everyone was afraid of, it is still growing today.

People want to think Jesus was here only to teach Love. He proved it when he married Mary Magdalene. His followers could see it. Man learned much more from Mary after Jesus was tortured and killed. They learned about woman which was not accepted before that happened. She did finish teaching Jesus students about God.

If anyone of you could look in Jesus' eyes you would be different. If you were ready for spirit to fill you, that went for anyone.

I was with Mary Madeline weeks before He was killed and the last days of His physical life. His teaching about death were beyond any teachings today and I can only touch on that until you experience it. Talking about dreams is just that. Experience is what anyone can hold on to.

His final teachings are called the secret teaching for a reason. He doesn't have to come back again to tell them again. People are still not ready yet. Jesus truly thought man would keep His truth growing instead of hiding it and pulling away from it. The race for power still has power over the world.

Now, people are talking about spirituality and awareness like they know why they are important. They are leaving out GOD and attributing the power to the universe. Which is only on the lowest plane of soul's journey.

Why do you think Jesus was so angry in the temple? They had the ark of the covenant there. It should have not been there.

It was not about selling in church. More important was having the highest recognized Priests ignorant to truth. I really think most Christians are blind to who Jesus really was as well.

I need to pull in the teaching and ideas of Ezekiel's vision now. Whatever they were I cannot say I was not with him during it. The truth is it had nothing to do with a real GOD.

If you go to any UFO seminar and listen to ten people's story they will be much better than his vision in the Bible. So, are you going to except them as real? Even mine are better. I can prove them to myself. They pertain to a real God not just to a Deity, angel or demon. It is not a fake story to make everything feel better.

People are dealing with stories, created out of someone's programmed mind as to what God must be and now ponder if He is an alien? That usually means not real. If God is in the story it must include God as being Love. The Ten commandments did not have the word love in it.

Where was Moses coming from again? Black magic relates to sacrifice, killing and sex. Moses was trying to control everyone more than anyone else on this planet at that time, while he was preaching to them about freedom.

Out of his six-hundred and thirteen laws, one sick law of an evil-minded man is known as niddad. A law of purity for a woman to get married.

Man doesn't have to prove it ever, never did. I can tell you 98% of men are not a virgin and would not want to say that either unless they are Jewish. There is a way to prove men are virgins as well but man's sick ego would never let that happen and be exposed. Man would have to agree to do it.

Paul was also not one of the twelve disciples. He never saw Jesus in the flesh.

He saw Jesus in a vision. Why is it very few people believe anyone's vision now? They did then. There are many visions now and none of them offer anything important to the world.

Why is that? What's up?

We had John the Baptist who spent his life in service to Jesus. Jesus declaring him the greatest man alive born of a woman not an alien.

He was killed by a bcheading. Is anything happening sound like love yet? No, don't worry it will never be just that. Not on planet earth. Not for another one-hundred years unless a serious destruction occurs.

The truth hurts more than a lie. A lie usually makes you feel good. Then if you believe it you will stay happy for a while. Sooner or later on your dying bed you will ask where is that happiness? Hopefully not the idea of floating around like a star in the universe.

They called Jesus a Rabbi. Do you know most Rabbis are married? All Jesus disciples were married. Why was the Priesthood not allowed to get married years later? The same people that started rewriting Jesus's truth, which they did not understand, had to create something for control.

Truth of Mary M

As I get closure to what Jesus was really teaching I am building every reason why it would be true and not just another story or lie.

The people around Jesus were mostly poor people. The rich always had everything they wanted already. The proof they needed was much different. They wanted to hear something and decide how real it sounded to them. His disciples became true believers. Even with proof, the rich still did not want to believe.

Why would anyone want to build a castle without a foundation? That foundation was and always is God. As you see that disappear so will humanity.

I will repeat three times in this book. The same as in the Bible. Jesus spoke about "it is easier for a camel to go through an eye of a needle then a rich person to get into heaven". Do you think many people (rich) will give most of their money up for something outside their home? I am not talking about people that are rich that give a million or so to charity. Then they take it off their income tax. It makes them look like a good person.

It took two thousand years for them to even tell a small part of the truth about Mary Magdalene. It happened in our lifetime they allowed that truth out while many still don't accept any of it. The Priesthood did not allow any woman to have any real kind of power, many Priests will not accept it or talk about it. They did not write about that in their Bible.

My truth, from being there, not that it was ever written. It is about how powerful Mary really was. She was incredible. Jesus' mission rested on her not Mary the mother of Jesus. She had the final responsibility to finish the teaching to all Jesus' followers.

Many of His followers did not get to understand it from Jesus. If He had more time He could have finished it. Mary found it even harder to teach men. They were so against any woman in power. I can only give you my truth.

When things were getting scary, like Governing royalty-power gaining control. Fear started growing no matter how many times Jesus told them if they give their life for God they will have eternal life.

Right now, how many people would really give their lives up for God? They might give it up for a lie. How is that even possible?

Many other teachings talk about reaching the bliss state or being in heaven. That would be giving up everything that you truly are. That is nothing to what to what God allows you to be. I call that soul and it has its own awareness even without the mind. If only you can get mind to allow itself to listen to soul you would know everything you ever wanted to know plus more.

Jesus was giving the secret teachings near His end times. He did have a few of his followers understand it. They were the ones Jesus sent around the world.

Mary Magdalene was gifted as well as carrying Jesus child. It was during the same time that the people were getting ready to kill Jesus. She was a priestess with the powers of Jesus. She was always one step ahead of the armies that were searching for her.

Please understand Jesus knew everything that was going to happen as well. He knew He had to die for His own teaching to be understood.

Spirituality has no connection to love. All people on this planet will differ. The idea of love is individualized. Very few people relate love directly to God. They would rather deal with relating to man's idea of It. If you go into higher vibration and energy you will not be thinking do I love you or that? You will never gain that ability until you learn about GOD Itself.

Man's ignorance in thinking he is so important to God, really, in his state of consciousness? Man thinks his deeds and actions create the universe. Man is ignoring what he is really doing to this planet and the ones around us. While men remove everything about God.

Take away sex, toys, drinking, sports, cheap thrills and relationships. Take away your cars, your planes and even some of the animals like your cats and dogs, what do you think would matter?

If you start understanding what God really gave us, you would see what we can become. It is awareness, not of mind or body but of spirit the true connection to God.

Mary M. had a very hard life after Jesus was killed. She now had to hide her daughter and go underground. Once the population realized what was happening after Jesus was now gone, the armies tried to kill anyone following or talking about Jesus teachings.


Why?


Were they talking about love of spirit? No, it was about being immortal. It was about leaving the lower worlds and moving into the higher realms. That alone takes away other people's power over you.

It was beyond the physical and that really scared them, the people in power.

It was the same at wounded Knee when the Calvary killed all the woman and children. When they thought about the Ghost Dance it brought fear to them.

Jesus was trying to teach people about how and why they came to this planet. It was not about how many children you could bring into this world which many religions make it out to be.

Each race did come from different worlds. There are nine races in all, of the races we call human. There were only four races left on this planet after the death of Atlantis.

All records of Atlantis disappeared and new writings were put in place. Aliens were part of the rebuilding of a society that they wanted to create (killers and farmers). They wanted the killers but needed the farmers. Different races all had different abilities. They were not supernatural just simple abilities. They were the abilities that could be used for their needs.

Whether you believe in the Bible, Emerald tablets, Quran, Samarian tablets, the book of Urantia or not. There are simple things that you cannot deny. How much truth about soul did they have?

How people lived was always controlled. The Hindu people gave their alliance to Deities. Whether you except them as little Gods or not they were also controlling the people. You have many wars going on, Aliens vs. the little Gods, Gods vs. Demons.

I want you to think why, out of them all real demons and the devils seemed to have disappeared. They are just passed off as bad souls in the psychic and new age world. They talk about becoming sixth dimensional Beings.

At the same time, any reference to God had changed to a power source. That was because people grew further away from God and what it really was.

Man has been selling out his own soul just as people talk about selling their soul to the devil. Man is doing it unconsciously. Man's desires are now earthly. His desires have nothing to do with what Jesus was teaching.

The idea of going back into kindergarten after graduating collage is not a very realistic idea, is it?

To be on a dying planet where man is creating more dieses then they are curing yearly. They are releasing more toxins, and destroying all our food at every level. Man thinks he is becoming spiritual. Where eating dolphins and whales are excepted.

What Jesus said was always taken to the level of the people at that time. Just as if you were having a conversation with Tesla how much do you think you would understand? All Jesus teachings were beyond planet earth they were not just how to live here.

He did say a few simple things like you live by the laws you make. When they are no longer right you change them. The laws of God are what you always need to follow. It was not if you did not like the Ten Commandments make a new set.

Man was a thief. The British took the constitution of the Native people. They killed them and then used their constitution for the rights of white people coming into the U.S.

The so called caring people like Jefferson while making peace with some tribes, he went on the road across the US killing every Native tribe he could. Washington gave the orders to kill many tribes. He made ever tribe think he was their friend. The day he signed a peace agreement with one tribe he would give the orders to kill another. You must realize fifty million Native people were killed in four hundred years.

Jesus never spoke about how to kill or murder, neither did people like Gandhi. Most all other leaders gave the orders to kill. Does that make it right? Never.

Jesus spoke about if you get hit on the left side of your face turn you face and let them hit the other side. He never said what came after that.

As man was growing in his own truth Jesus' teachings became different. It was no longer what Jesus was really teaching. How do people come to a place where killing is still ok and justified? Abuse keeps growing.

All religions say they follow their laws. Do you think any religion follows their true teaching? On Moses' laws, do you think anyone on this planet could live by Moses six-hundred and thirteen laws? Moses could not live by ten.

The first and most important law would be about eating. They are forced to eat things they should not by their own law. Jesus said which I will repeat, "it is not what you put in the body it is what comes out of it".

They hid from the words they could not understand. The same as when Jesus spoke about rebirth they could only perceive giving birth again in a physical way to another child. They never understood eternal life in a spiritual way.

Man, now makes it sound like they can just wash away everything that happened in their life. It was called baptism and it was about cleansing the mind. Jesus started giving them as much truth as he could, He could no longer wait until they were ready.

Risen - getting ready to leave the lower worlds

Mary the mother of Jesus was always around us during the preparation of the Crucifixion. Why do you think she was always in back round of Mary Magdalene? After Jesus had risen, He appeared first to Mary M. She was the first to talk to Him when He came back to our reality. He was in his astral body.

Many of His followers did not understand the astral body. It is the next body soul will take after the physical dies. That form was used so they could know it was really Jesus. Jesus was already moving into a higher body.

Everyone moves into the astral body for a time. There are three ways to go up to the next plane. One is stay where you are. Two is or reincarnate back to earth. Three is moving past the astral plane.

Jesus' physical ability was incredible. Why He was tortured so long and could not stop it? He had to die. His disciples would not have followed Him if He did not come back to meet with them, all His teaching would have been in vain.

There are many stories created by Aliens. With the truth about time travel they could see where their teaching was going and able to change it at any given time. That is not in an effective way.

Something to show you, is true is out - of -place artifacts. That meaning things that cannot be in a certain place because it did not exist there at that time.

They are finding a new pyramid about every six months now. Why are they not talking about what they are finding inside them?

Did Jesus speak about Myths? Why would he have to? They already believed in so many remarkable stories that came out of so-called visions.

Out of all the tribal stories very few were important or even real. I am not sure any really were based on where we are at today. Man has only increased his technology not his spirituality, awareness or ability to love.

When someone teaching history, he is teaching by hypothesis. They have very little actual proof, which most history is just that, his-story.

All stories about space are just theories. There is no real proof of anything beyond earth and the moon. Pictures are all we have and even that is being recreated at every level.

Jesus never spoke of the past. He was not teaching other people's teachings. He did not repeat stories. He did not have to. With all his followers, how many of His teachings made it to today? All you can hear in any church is all that matters is love. I will say that over and over.

Would any mother allow their son to die for God? I don't think so. They will let them die for the U.S. as every other country does it as well. How sick is that?

When Jesus was being arrested and was in prison how many ran and had to hide? His own followers allowed Jesus to be killed, why? They were only worried about their reality. They did not even know what that meant at that time. Give up everything, they would ask themselves why? Walk away from their family, why? Do people today even understand that? Do people wonder why Jesus did not have to teach anything about love? Simply He showed it.

Jesus was a bringer of truth; how many were willing to listen? If He ever did come back what would people expect to hear? We are all saved? We are all going to heaven? We are all forgiven? For what? If you don't except karma what do you know about paying it off? The lies one told, the people that they hurt, the people they abused, the woman and men they cast to the wayside, the child they did not treat fair, The people they cursed and ridiculed.

Or the fact they never even wanted to find .
the truth themselves.

Many stories came out a hundred or
two hundred years later. Then who is
telling that story, Constantine?

Back to me. After many years of
studying many different paths and now
closing in on what I feel is total truth.
Twenty-five years studying with a
Medicine woman, I spent twenty years
with Eckankar. I was with a Varjra master
for a few years. At the very end, it was to
the point of trying to commit suicide and
almost dying. I saw much deeper than
anyone I could even talk to.

The people that had near death
experiences had very little experience of
what really happens when one dies.
Saying how they went through the light
and seeing an angel or family member.
That is not even important when you are
working on trying to move into a higher

world. That is only the astral plane. Most of that is created by the mind.

I was becoming aware of my past lives a few a year. Going back to Atlantis. Which was the most beautiful time of planet earth for many eons. That was the only time I was truly happy.

Man was not growing from monkeys. There were different races the same as all the entities that lived here before and next to humanity.

Many of the souls that were here are still serving out their karma and still creating it. Earth's karma was nothing like it is now. Man keeps making earth karma harder to work off, while they live in the delusion they are religious.

Many new deities were being created by people in India way back in time. Their worlds were becoming sexual energy rather than spiritual energy. I suppose, no one was looking for what a real God of creation would really be. They accepted anything, everything that had power. If a so-called holy person would say I am all that you search for they would believe it. People except any vision from a "holy person" they get and feel it is true.

If any entity knows they have you they will not let you go. I mention how no one accepts demons are real and are here. People still can sell their souls.

I am watching everything worldwide, people going into the idea of being an experiencer. That just means an illusion dream, program or drug related experience. I would call it a bad dream which they call a good one. No matter how real it feels where does it really bring you?

People think they are so important that they had to return to planet earth to be a healer. Jesus did not come here to be a healer. The problem is that is what people wanted from their Teacher/healer, not how to experience God.

Kennedy was close when he said, "ask not what your country can do for you but what you can do for your country". He wanted to tell the people about aliens.

The Government did not want him to. The same as Marilyn Monroe wanted to speak about that as well. It was the downfall of both. That was only the start of killing more people to keep all that info quiet.  There is a reason for that.

Back to the main issue. Who was Jesus? Everything I say is coming from direct experience. It is from past life experience. I was with Mary M. She always dressed in incredible perfection. We dressed in blue. The color of the Goddess's of temple.

Everything they wrote about her was a story of three other people. They did not want to give any credibility to a woman. Being around her was always incredible. Looking in her eyes you could see the light. I never met any other woman that was like that in all my lifetimes. She did the things that Jesus did. You don't hear a thing about that in the Bible. The most important things that happened in all our histories completely stripped from all written words. Then filled with ever lie possible.

My heart was heavy because I was never able to get close to Mary's daughter, Sarah, she had to go into hiding. No other person could walk in her footstep then nor now. I wish I lived longer to see what she did in her life.

They were killing people just for practicing trivial things Jesus taught. That was different forms of meditation. The people in power looked at it as disrespect to their God.

I do want to back track about when I got baptized at fourteen and could ask my Minister three questions.

1.    What does God look like?

2.    What does God do?

3.    What does heaven look like?

He could not answer and said no one really knows. I walked away from my religion that day. I started my true search for truth. I still knew that I was connected to Jesus in some strange way.

I did not except stories ever. I became aware of many of my lives even the one before Atlantis and not on this planet.

## Birth of Sarah, many people know Her?

Mary having Jesus' child, I am sure all religionists have no idea what that's all about. A spiritual woman carrying the highest energy on this planet with a female child. Man could never deal with that. I cannot say much after Mary went underground. I did see Sarah before she left. Don't forget Mary had to finish teaching Peter the hardest to teach out of the disciples. Peter learned well.

After being in Atlantis, it's amazing how only two people ever spoke about it many years later. Socrates spoke about Atlantis from what he heard. It was not like any story people ever heard.

This is the truth I repeat there were nine races there. It was the only time planet earth was really the Garden of Eden. After five races reached spiritual awareness, they left, leaving four races. They were reprogrammed by a few different alien races after it was destroyed.

In Jesus' time, I was born in a rich family and later became a Goddess when many of my family were killed. My name was Maria and she Is mentioned in the Bible in a few places. I am talking about the first Bible.

There was very little information or stories about Jesus' childhood then. So how could there be much now? The few that knew Jesus, knew He was working with His family for brief time.

Mary asked me to come to her temple to meet Jesus. Jesus taught her everything before He left to go back out. Mary the mother of Jesus was a good friend to Mary M. She followed Mary M around as much as she could. She always walked behind her. She was never considered a spiritual being while she was alive. Now that she is dead she is placed as the highest taking away from everything that Mary M. was.

Mary M. was the one that had to go into hiding. There were already underground armies being formed to protect her and her daughter.

Jesus started teaching a few things which mankind doesn't even know now.

Jesus came to bring the most important message I have ever heard. People confused what He taught the public with what He taught His followers. You must realize people then were very simple people. They had only a few of the words we have now. Love was not even excepted the way it is now for much was forced on woman then.

Men were the power of the world then and even now it is very little different even though woman think it is. I guess being able to vote and go to war, gives woman more power in their thinking.

What Jesus was teaching the simple people was about compassion. Which was a little more understood then Love.

Men had very little love for woman.

It was always worse for female children. If they lived from abuse they were forced into marriage and sex. Many were used in many kinds of sacrifices.

There was no way Jesus taught love without showing it. He had to win the confidence of people. It was mostly the poor at first. When He made miracles suddenly everyone was listening. The Priesthood was afraid from the start that they could lose their power.

If Jesus did not heal people very few people would have believed Him or follow him. Again, He did not come here to be a healer. There was no one that could heal the dead. He healed the dead but not in the way it is written in the Bible. Their souls would rise to heaven. To reincarnate, not to live life the same as people without awareness live.

In the statement - Jesus said, "the living Father" a word used for the people who would know no other. About the true spiritual being, the word now used Is God.

The Living Father that had sent Him. He lived by that. Jesus says He that eat of Him shall live by Him. He was speaking about the bread of heaven. Again, something different than their idea of physical bread. There is a difference from a dream and action.

Jesus had to teach simple ideas for people to follow. He came to teach what is called the (secret teaching). That being something that most people would never understand.

He asked? What if you see the Son of Man ascend to where it was before? He did not go into detail to the public about heaven ever. He did teach his few disciples that understood what He was saying. Mary M was one of them and became His most important teacher. Why is that not in the Bible?

Why?

He said, "that is, the quickening." The flesh does not help it. He then says, "the word, are of spirit." (meaning from God). It is Not God. "They are Life." Meaning the life of Soul being eternal, not the physical body, we all are a soul realized or not.

John, doing the writing had a limited idea as well. He goes on about how Jesus knew who would portray him, and who were his true followers. That too was never correct in the Bible.

Many of His followers betrayed Him and even help kill Him. The story of Judas is one more lie. Judas was one of Jesus' closest followers next to Thomas.

Thomas was the smartest out of all His followers. Meaning the one that was always asking questions of Jesus. They gave him the wrong name of doubting Thomas.  Yes, proof is important.

Jesus had the hardest mission on this planet. That was to teach about death of the body and teaching to be aware of soul.

That is not what Buddha taught at all. Buddha spoke about the Mind as if it is important to what one really is.

Mind has no clue to past lives. It is the connection of soul feeding the mind that knowledge comes from. Mind only knows what it is programmed to. Every word it is taught has a program with it. It forms the ideas of what a person becomes. That only changes when mind learns to listen to soul and starts removing itself from Karma and the dogma of life. That is what Jesus did teach.

Jesus taught about Death in many ways. He had to show it to His followers for it to really sink in. He allowed them to see His soul rise into the heavens.

Much of what was shown was written differently in the Bible. For many of Jesus' followers had their own interpretation of what they heard. You have Mathew, Mark, Luke and John. What is even funnier is that two of them were evangelists. I would say they put their own take on things but in a twisted way. They are the ones to blame for the many of the lies in the new testament.

Jesus tells His followers that He will be with them a brief time and then He will return to what has sent Him here. After He is gone they will not be able to find Him. He says many times, "I tell you over and over and still you don't listen". He was forced to use methods that even the simple- minded people in the world could understand.

The Father is how they could relate to God. The Creator God, giving birth to Jesus. They had a challenging time understanding that.

How could He explain it was not Mary the mother of Jesus but an Angel of God that allowed His soul to step into this world, like we all do. That doesn't make it good or bad. That part is learned from their family, all their accumulated karma. It is very little about soul's true journey beyond planet earth. It is souls first steps on it's true path.

Only a few souls truly know much more than Nostradamus who was beyond the thinking of the men around him.

Today there are few souls with the knowledge of what Jesus had at any level. People think and say they know what Jesus taught but it was not Love and forgiveness.

It was about Karma, Reincarnation and soul's awareness of the higher realms. It was about the many worlds beyond the physical and astral. That alone is now being excepted as heaven.

Not anyone can get there no matter what they think. It is beyond where most people will have to wait to see how much karma they have worked off, to see if they can even stay on the astral plane.

The astral plane is not anything close to a real spiritual heaven. Heaven is misunderstood by people. Thinking just dying puts them in heaven. It will put your body in the ground.

Do you know there is no proof of Jesus' body anywhere other than the shroud of Terran? There are many theories. Every story about Jesus is so misunderstood. The people that wrote them had very little understanding of what He was really teaching. When Jesus died his followers thought their teachings did as well.

The first important thing about Jesus' teaching is there was no other person teaching here about what He taught.

There were many twisted lies and false ideas. The world was always about power and money. The idea of what money is keeps changing and it is about to change again. It's nothing good.

Rulers were being controlled by deities and aliens. Love was a none existent idea. Present day man came up with another useless concept called unconditional Love. It means nothing to this world, it has zero energy to do what people think it does. Heal the planet, man and woman really? What about the sick, starving and homeless? Does it give them energy from God? Only God could do that.

Jesus was teaching compassion. His love and compassion for Mary M was incomparable to any other. Knowing He would never see His daughter in the physical, He knew they both would live in very dangerous times when He was gone.

The world would have never heard the true story if Mary did not live for a long-time teaching Jesus' truth. Leaving her teaching with her daughter. The true teachings did survive. Remember what Jesus said, He could do what His father could do. That came from the man side of Jesus. That was limited to the physical and astral level.

Jesus felt He had to bring out His truth. It was all about saving one's soul from the cycle of reincarnation over and over. Not staying in it. Many paths except reincarnation as a way of life.

The first real teachings after Jesus was killed was brought out in small parts through paths from Sufi and Shabd yoga masters, before that the Whirling Dervishes. They were now trying to bring God down to Earth and that started only a few hundred years ago. It was now using physical exercises to reach enlightenment which was only one part of Jesus teaching.

He was teaching how to become aware of soul. It is beyond mind and the physical world.

If one experiences soul very few souls would look back a second time. Just as Lot told his wife not to look back. Did she listen? Of course not.

The stories had to relate to normal living. He spoke about dreams, day dreaming, trances, astral projection, and even speaking in tongue. He explained about all the psychic abilities and the downfall of them. They each have different energies with them. He spoke with Lucifer and He had to teach about that. Man did create their own reasons about that.

Jesus had to deal with the darkness for a long time. (forty nights?) Which is what all people will have to do in this life or if not their next life. The time will be different for the level that one is trying to get to and what they already really learned.

If you tear apart the Bible you will see very little spiritual truth. He spoke about giving this world what it deserves and giving God what It deserves. Do people know what that is? It is not sitting, praying for hours. It is not about having sex for six hours. It is not about physical things.

Spirituality has little connection to this world. It's amazing how people (wish) and want it to be what they think it should be. Spiritual and religious are man-made words for a man's ego.

Jesus clamed very little other than His father (GOD) sent him. He truly never said He was God.

In the statement saying Jesus said His father and I are one. I never heard Him say that. He was not saying He was God ever. No, He was saying He lived within all God's laws and within It's love. That love is not like what people are searching for here.

People now care about living long. The longer the better. That has nothing to do with what Jesus was teaching. Nothing.

As I go deeper into Jesus teachings you will see everything He taught was about. The death of the body and becoming aware of soul. It's learning first how to be true to spirit.

If a person speaks about finding truth, what one needs to know will not come from books but by experience.
Early Christians came from a line of killers. The same as it happened then and is still happening now. When the white man came to America, or where ever they went they were killers.

Something important is that you will never get another person to truly understand your truth. What most People's truth is really a programmed idea?

I know many people will not except what I am saying because of the deep programming they have, that was fed to them all their life.

What makes something someone said a long time ago more important then what something someone says now? What proof do they have now? What is the difference of either? It's simple, very few people have proved their teaching. They don't even have a way for a person to prove it to themselves.

God real or not?

I did not know Jesus all His life. I do know that He went to learn His truth inside a pyramid. He went through ascension* there. We have many people saying they went through it now, except not one word they say can prove it. Many people do not understand it.

When Jesus came back He had learned the thirty-two psychic abilities that come from the higher part of the astral plane. People on earth had them for a very long time during Atlantis. They were taken away after Atlantis was destroyed.

When you are dealing with God's energy nothing can really hurt you. You (meaning), soul. The body is a victim of the laws of this world. Soul is protected so it cannot get hurt unless it allows it to happen.

Soul does learn as it moves through different life's and the bodies. There are four bodies it uses after the one let's go of the physical one. The last body called the true soul body can be dropped when that awareness is reached.

At that point, you are letting go of what many deities are still holding on to forms with power.

Do you really think you need to pray to God for hours days and years? Do you think you know what God created the world for? There are many different life forms.

A roach or an ant is a life form most people don't understand. They don't change. Their life is always simple. The earth changes trivial things in their life. Most do not have the ability to change things. Just because a roach can change its body to fit the environment doesn't mean it is learning anything different.

You need to ask yourself right now. Why do most speakers speak about getting everything you need in life? A home, a car, a decent job and children. At the same time Jesus told his disciples to leave everything including their families and friends. People in religion never look at anything they don't like or understand. Such as what things one can do that cannot be forgiven.

In Jesus' time, they had no idea of karma even though it was part of everyone's life. Jesus spoke about going out and not committing the acts you know are wrong. If you are not told something is wrong, you really don't know it is. It is in the programming children get now. Why is it they get no real spiritual truth? They would know right and wrong right away. Man did not decide that for himself.

I am not speaking about religious programming. I am sure you think I am contradicting everything I am saying.

Jesus never used the word spiritual. His people would not understand it anyway. Now people just make up their ideas about truth as they go along.

I do not look at truth as being religious or spiritual. When you get into the higher worlds or planes you can use the word spiritual. The more you know about God the more you understand the word, not before.

Morals are only the first level. Most people have very little or no morals. At the same time, morals are disappearing more and more every day.

Jesus was dealing with His own people attacking Him as well as outsiders. He had to try to get his twelve followers to learn something they had no understanding about.

The Egyptians had a few ideas about life after death. They did not have enough knowledge to know that you do not come back into the same body. They did know about reincarnation in some way. Why would anyone except any story that was older than that one and think it is real?

Going back another one thousand years before the birth of Jesus, the people of India's first named religion were dealing with the deities. They were also real while they were not God. They were the higher souls and protectors of the lower worlds.

I had my first experience with a deity at the age six for five years. At twelve my mother told me spirits are not real. It took me two years and going through baptism to get back into my true spiritual search. I then left Christianity. It was when I was about twenty-eight that I found out what deity I was really dealing with when I was younger.

Proving to yourself

I want to talk about a past life experience. I was only about ten. I had a strange dream. It was about a relationship I was in. It was a relationship with a Japanese woman. I never saw a woman completely nude before that. I made love to her. I woke up soaked and crying. Not understanding what was really happening. I knew people kissed. Nothing more than that.

I was a sheltered beaten child. So, after that my desire to always be with a woman started growing. That sexual act did not happen until years later in the physical. I was with my first wife.

I don't want to go into my reason for coming back in this lifetime now. There is still too much to speak about.

I had three marriages and eight relationships in my life. Three of them I had serious problems with having a child. Three made sure the child that was coming died or did not.

Love and God was and is my heart's desire. I always said I will do anything once. Jesus came into my life at a very early age. Not as a story. I perceived Him as a brother or close friend. He allowed me to re-live my past life.

After twenty-five I had two direct experiences with God. I had a few with Jesus in his world not mine. That means being on or in the third world. Where He was at that time. He was teaching there.

When a person calls on Jesus, do you think He will come back here for anyone that calls His name? That is called wishful thinking. Would you listen even if He did? I know many people say they spoke to God. I will not debate that here. People speaking to Jesus, what do you think they ask or what questions does Jesus answer? How many people are touching the truth about why they are here? They just want to survive.

People in religions with ideas are of a false heaven or fake one. What are people thinking, what will be their rewards for living? Nothing we have here can come with us when we leave, except what we learned or did not learn.

I never heard anything different then the programmed idea of love and protection people have. If we are all going into higher dimension the world needs to move into the Golden age. Many things need to happen first.

I am having a very hard time just waking up to see if the world is still here.

We are being forced not to be prejudice. That must mean a person is supposed to be brain dead. Being forced to except one sick person's ideas.

How can any person saying that they are (spiritual) or even a caring person when they don't or cannot see that a few religions are evil? They are evil to their own people never mind to the entire world. They just sit back and say we are supposed to except it. I am not talking about going out and killing them. I guess the same kind of people made sure Jesus was killed. I am not talking about Judas either.

If you had a choice to come now or in a thousand years, if the world makes it into the golden age, which would you want to come into? Most people will take the path of so called (least resistance). It's not the road of pain.

Talk to weight lifters doing their daily routine. One works to the end of his limits and the other stops when he feels a little tired.  Who do you think will reach what they both want?

Spiritual truth as Jesus taught is the hardest path soul will take to get out of the lower worlds. Most men cannot let go of the cheap thrills, the sex the fun. I guess man will stay in this world and will allow it to crumble.

Do you think Jesus was not real? Well that is your choice. Jesus was not as important as people think the Pope is today.

The Pope is rewriting two of Ten Commandments and not willing to tell the people the truth of what is really happening. He is telling his followers there is no such thing as hell and why it was created, calling it all lies. That is while he is living in it. He is calling the story of Adam and Eve fake. It was a story about a small part of truth. Man was created, not hatched.

In all the teaching and stories no one is telling the truth about where man came from.

Worse is that no one is speaking about the truth of soul. When Jesus brought up soul, He was speaking to a very sedated race of people when it came to awareness. It was never understood before.

The Hindu people spoke about creating energy that puts you in with the Gods or source's energy. A true God doesn't need sex. It is not male or female.

When Jesus said my father, he was not speaking about a man. He was creating a connection to something that very few people will ever truly understand. It is two thousand years later and people are still trying to understand the idea of God. They are not trying to understand what IT truly is, just what they want it to be.

It is easy to dream and even harder to dream outside the box. The box is just what it sounds like. In Jesus' teaching, it was about the soul body. Its functions are totally different then the physical body, that soul is only using temporarily.

There are entities outside the norm such as demons that affect people from moving forward at any great speed. Right now, we are seeing the collapse of all human morals. The deteriorations of families and the creation of children. Who are void of compassion and real connection. You could call it the Zombie world. All of this is being created in a test tubes right now.

When Jesus spoke about the worlds of God the only way you would know them to be real is by actual experience. The truth and how it worked was described in the Bible by Paul/Saul.

Paul met with Jesus after Jesus' physical body was killed. He was now dealing with the soul of the astral world. Jesus spoke about how he has not yet ascended. He explained about soul leaving the body the light and even the body's own light. He spoke of how the colors of the light show the awareness of soul itself.  Art took on a new form from that.

Let me bring up one very important point now, many people talk about forgiveness because of a line in the Lord's Prayer. What does that have to do with God forgiving people? What is forgiveness to people in the first place? People think it is their right to be in heaven.

All souls go to the astral plane when the body dies, including murderers. Then they are placed where they deserve to go from there. There are three levels there as well. Only a few get to stay there. There are the ones that don't go. Their called ghost or spirits.

Forgiveness is a man-made concept to think one can be cleared from all the wrong things they did from someone else.

Do you understand God? I am sure you don't. Why would IT have to forgive anything, especially anything that IT created. It can do whatever IT wants to, destroy a city or country of people. I am not sure how people come up with forgiveness with that one! IT does however relate to all the karma everyone has together.

Forgiveness is an excuse for man's own fear of facing the things he did or does. Why would God have to forgive a rapist? It would not have to and doesn't. I am sure God is not happy at all when It sees what man is creating.

Jesus was very compassionate. If you understand God, you start understanding yourself. Which only a few souls ever do.

It is different from when Jesus spoke about the many rooms in His father's mansion. It meant many levels and planes of existence. So, do you think a rapist would go to any higher plane?

Hell, is here so it is only a matter of learning how to leave it not how to stay here in it. That is the beginning of what

Jesus was teaching. He was not teaching heaven is here and now. One must have a very sick idea of heaven to believe that.

If one looks at this world as heaven they are very sick and limited in understanding God or even the idea being spiritual. Yes, the world could be a lot closer to being spiritual. That would mean seven billion people working together not in a dream, but in the physical reality. That is not going to happen any time soon. Unless something like the Day the Earth stood still happened.

The angels get involved with all the trivial things like moving souls around, not God. If man really thinks he is that important, guess again.

Why does man think God is worried about if he is going to be a bartender or plumber or become a king? Each level of jobs has a certain ego with it or lack of one. Police and Government being the worsts. Each have a certain karma associate with it.

Jesus was not here to make people change their life, just learn what it means and how to live within it, then more important where one goes after it. He was not here to take on the sins of the world. Most people that are not Christians don't even care, if that is even true, which it isn't. They know the truth but that truth that only reflects the programming from the people around them that was man created.

I have been listening to people saying they are spiritual or religious for many years and the only thing I hear is their ego. Why is it no one really speaks about God?

WHY?

If you have no idea of what I am speaking about, I will make it simple. If one race kills fish and birds for food, another kills people for food, another doesn't kill any creatures for food who is right or spiritual? What if an alien race from another world liked to eat people? Would they be wrong?

People that don't understand anything about Jesus. They don't have any understanding of spiritual laws.

If one doesn't understand God, they have no understanding of any spiritual worlds other than the astral plane. I do not include the astral world with the spiritual world ever. It is not much better there. The souls there are still in kindergarten compared to people in collage. Schools have no understanding of anything spiritual or teach anything about truth. They cannot even teach children real morals. What they do teach is how to make money and live without truth.

Many of the followers or people around Jesus were farmers and sellers of farm goods. They did not need much more than food and a roof over their head.

They did have their bars and sex dens. They also had arenas and the armies that were killers. The builders were always working for the people in power. The slaves had very little chance to meet Jesus or follow any religion.

Jesus' disciples were still dealing with the idea of praying to something they knew nothing about while trying to relate to Jesus Himself. It became easy for them while He was alive and doing all the miracles.

When it came to cities fighting over whether Jesus was a savoir, they started pulling deeper inside themselves. They were afraid to follow someone that the high society were now attacking and afraid of.

With all Mary's abilities, it was still incredibly hard to keep Jesus' teachings alive. It did help the men understand family when she had Jesus's daughter.

Mary the mother of Jesus was not there much after Jesus was killed. She did not ever have the abilities Mary M. possessed. Her job was to bring Jesus into this world. That was it. Mary Magdalene's mission was to finish bringing Jesus' teaching out to the world.

Jesus met with the disciples every day, giving His discourse to them. Starting with what death means to soul. Man did not hear words like reincarnation, astral travel, out-of- body experiences. Now words like soul body reflect so much more of what Jesus was teaching.

Spiritual Laws in the physical

When one dies, they become more alive than they have ever been. Things that mattered in this world hopefully fade away. If one is starting to understand the spiritual laws, understands this, there are few spiritual laws in the physical realms. Here they are.

#1. The law of non-interference.

#2. The law of there is only one God.

#3. The law of silence. Listening to God, not telling IT what to do.

#4. The law of disobedience. That is the law of karma. Live by the law and die by it. It has nothing to do with manmade laws.

#5. The law of truth. All will face it in their judgment time. What one does one will be accountable to that.

#6. Gods' Love. One needs to truly understand to learn what and who God really is. What IT's love means.

When Jesus spoke, one must realize that the same as in today's times, everyone has their own ideas and how many are the same as everyone else's?

When Jesus said, "Unless one comes as a child they will never see the face of God". Have you ever wondered or realized, when you were very little, who was the first one you ever loved next to your mother and father? Did it have to do with any ideas of race, color, looks or money? What did it really involve? There were things, like dolls, blankets, pets and even God.

Children are the closest to true love and it gets taken away as the years go by. It gets built into something so different. The opposite of the real feeling and yes sex becomes a big part of it.

There are six basic laws that people don't want to except. You can live by your laws or God laws. Your laws will keep you reincarnating over and over whether in this world or any of the other ones. One will have to learn God's laws before they ever get out of the lower realms. Man's laws create karma daily.

When Jesus was trying to teach about ascending* as people try to today, it was no better then. The people trying to teach it have no clue to what it really means.

Man, wants everything given to him. He is not willing to work for it. That work is not of the physical world. Many people think the opposite. You can kill people here. You cannot do that on the astral plane. You must eat here but you don't have to eat there. We eat to keep the body alive. It doesn't matter to man what they kill to eat.

Soul is of light and High vibrations. It stays sustained on the light and sound of God that comes down through all worlds to here, also called spirit. It is not the sun. The light is not as strong as when it is in the higher worlds. Soul doesn't need physical food like a body does. Tesla was taught relating energy to that idea. How he created free energy and even time travel.

The laws of a body in the physical are so different than in the astral body. It changes when soul goes beyond the astral plane to the third world or realm.

When Jesus spoke to people they were not dealing with alternate realities, inter-dimensional, hyperspace, holograms, or even the Astral plane. The programming had already started about heaven and hell though.

All through history there were so called spiritual people. The further you go back in time the more these people insisted their teaching came from aliens or deities. The poor definition of God today is still useless. It has no truth about what God is.

Words like super powerful, all knowing and eternal are not even one percent of what IT is or can do. Christian beliefs take away from what God is even more. Man, relates Jesus to that.

I am reluctant to say this to people, Jesus was a man. He could use the Psychic abilities from the Astral plane but that did not make Him God.

In Atlantis people used them all. When the nine races were there, it was the only time they were all being used together.

There are three basic ones. Thirty-two useable ones and now people classify about a one-hundred more. Today there are only a few people that can use about six percent of these abilities. It is amazing not one person is close to being even twenty-five percent in tune.

Not one person can predict one minute in advance. There is major reason for that if you understand what man has already done with time travel that changed everything to this dimension. This including allowing entities into this reality that were not here before. All this has nothing to do what Jesus did.

Predicting something psychically for someone usually means that one thinks their truth is important for another. That is the opposite of the truth. Anything in the physical is only for the physical.

If you don't know what abilities I am talking about here are a few examples remote viewing, channeling, speaking in tongue, talking to spirits, astral projection, levitation, bio-location, prophecy and clairvoyance.

A word I don't like to use for most people is healing. I will say there are always nine spiritual people on the planet at any given time. Not that I have heard or met one. You can hear people talking about it. I am not speaking about fake healers who even believe it themselves.

Healings happen when people go to a so-called healer. By no means does it come from the person saying they are the healer. Second to that, what one thinks they get from another is only temporary.

Jesus never said He was God. He did things that only someone from another world could do in people's eyes.

Many people claimed to be psychic even at that time. Their knowledge was based on seeing the natural laws of this planet. Knowing the sun and moon phases are good examples, also the same as knowing when creatures will come out after years.

Planet earth is in the worst shape it has ever been in. Too many people followed the so-called psychics and what they said. That goes for all Native tribes. It was a shame the real psychics were never listened to. If they were, they were killed and given a name like witch or evil.

Now, we have all the new agers coming out saying they are connecting to every alien race and angles. They say that they have the truth now. No one has shed any proof that it is helping mankind. If it's not aliens and angels it is demons.

Angels have never come here to teach. They always came with major events and warnings of things going to happen.

Miracles are the workings of the devil in many cases. One might not see it that way. If God wants you and you feel like staying here who is right?

When Jesus spoke, He would say over and over why do you not understand My words? "I tell you, repeatedly, and you still do not listen". (what were they not doing)? They were not understanding anything He was saying about truth.

The truth He left with us, was the idea of rebirth in a higher world or realm.

In the end times, wars of countries against countries, famines, earth quakes, pestilences, betrayals of one and other, the false prophets all shall rise and deceive the world. Love will turn cold.

If one says, Christ is here, it is only their belief. For Jesus said, "He will be nowhere to be found here nor there". Look all you want. When the sun becomes dark, the moon becomes dark and the stars fall from the heavens this will be the end of times. I feel in every bone in my body it will be soon.

Jesus never said anything about Himself other then, He is of whom that has sent Him. God would not have to ever say that if IT was here.

If you stood before a deity no one would have to tell you what it was or is. Nothing in any of the two lower worlds have that kind of vibration, not even all the people together on this planet. If you have a big ego you might think different.

In Jesus' teachings was a concept now called meditation, then it was called connection. Connecting to the sound current and the light. Listening and seeing with the Inner eye also called the third eye. Which most people did not understand. The Hindu people spoke about it. In the oldest days' man used occultist and seers to do their bidding on things such as wars.

George Washington was doing remote viewing on his enemies, during the wars in New Your City. Then they moved to NJ where the first army base was built.

Do angels work with people? The ones that work with individuals have a very important message. If it is not about earth, soul must be ready to leave. It's funny, all the people saying they are working with angels without one important piece of information.

In most death experiences, people have very little true awareness from the experience. It's always about one's ego and the programming a person went through.

I had over five death experiences. I have listened to hundreds of people speaking about their experiences. What I will tell you, most relate to it with mind and they cannot relate to it as Soul.

Learning to travel begins with understanding the difference between the physical and the Astral Planes. After that you can start with the planes beyond them.

Jesus had a tough time teaching a few of His followers to astral travel. Many could not get past the astral plane into the worlds beyond. Something that's important, no one will ever get to a world they don't deserve.

There are a few important physical exercises. This is based on the idea that some people pray on their knees. There are a few steps toward the right way to do it.

There is a complete exercise to do, to align the body with the spirit. Which is the way Jesus ascended into the pyramid. Realize you don't have to be physically inside the pyramid. You can be there in a different dimension.

Very few people truly understand Heaven. It is not like earth in any way. In the planes beyond the astral, there is no fear, no hate, not pain, no lying, no sex as we know it and no solid food.

Jesus said, "it is not what you put in your body it is what comes out of it". I will repeat that again. That means your actions, words and light you radiate.

There are more colors, more sounds, everything is much brighter and louder there. You don't have eyes and ears like you do here. If you were in a human body it would explode.

There are stories about beings coming here in two separate forms. The stories of the two get mixed. One being physical and the other being spirit.

What is sad to me is people thinking that they are God or that they are equal to God. While they are not even equal to the lower Deities or the lowest angels.

Even now, psychics have very little abilities compared to what the people had in Atlantis. I would bet the ones saying that they have the most have the least abilities. Back in time the so-called prophets or psychics, it was easier to make people believe that they had super powers. The ones that claim to be psychics are taking money from desperate people who need help.

Jesus told His followers over and over that He was not going to be around long, which they could not understand. People need to be under the control of something. They think have spiritual powers. Like the wording in the Bible, unless you become like sheep will you ever see the face of God. Jesus did not write that.

The truth on how a spiritual person thinks is different than the way most people think.

People are trying to live longer and longer. They want to be smarter. There are two new pills that will help man think better and become that. It is expensive. What would smarter be? How long would longer be? As of right now man cannot live past one-hundred and twenty-five years. Smart is based on man's knowledge called IQ. That means how you deal with earth knowledge and programmed ideas that are accepted.

Imagine giving a person a spiritual IQ would anyone pass it? Having a death experience doesn't make you spiritual, it only makes you more aware if you can understand it.

There is no test for being spiritual yet, unless it is what man thinks psychic powers are.

Being psychic does not mean being spiritual. Many bad or negative people use it more than spiritual people do. Why? They speak about the programmed idea of love, compassion and their ability to make money. One can even kill with it, as Moses and Washington did. If you know Washington's story.

The people around Jesus that started understanding His teachings were told to go out into the world. Once that happened it was an all-out war starting with the Romans. They did not want people to become spiritual. It would cause them to lose power and control over the people. They could not allow it. They were out to kill them all.

So how did the Bible become the number one book? All the stories that were lies were added to it by man to control man.

Man doesn't want the truth. He will pay anything for lies. It just needs to sound good. The same person will pay nothing for the truth. It was always about control so why would it be any different now when it was then?

Mary's Daughter (Sarah) changed many things. She was now the carrier of Jesus power. As the armies against the disciples started getting bigger they went into hiding or they would all have been killed before any truth got out.

There were many years between Sarah taking her full power at the death of Mary Magdalene.

Sarah's army was called the knights of Templar. They built four pyramids for her. I cannot say what happened later. I do know most were killed. I cannot say I lived in that timeframe.

I am trying to fill in the details now of how Sarah died or where she disappeared to. The teaching is still here, but it is hidden. They are about learning how to rise past the astral plane. Working off your last bit of karma.

With seven point two billion people, only a few have a high mission which most people don't want to hear.

Reincarnation is a bitch. People want to believe that the idea of their mission is important but it consists of mental constructs.

Everyone has a mission if you want to call it that. I call it just living for most. Do you lead more people to spirit or take them away from it? If it has anything to do with the physical it is taking them away from it.

Man, wants to think we are all equal. In all planes, there is always something that separates one soul from another and is not taught in any man-made religion.

Jesus was the light they had to see. His voice was the sound they had to hear. It was not in a word, just the vibration of His voice or the star of His eyes or being able to be in His aura. That is spirit speaking through the body.

If you were aware in that time you could see the light coming down the streets before Jesus got to where you were. His light was so bright and that is why He was always shown with a white or yellow halo.

The high Priests had their magicians or witches to for-tell predictions. It was their egotistical thinking that made them think they were always better than everyone else.

For a teacher, not to be rich was not common. Jesus traveled with very little. Today you would say he had nothing except the clothes He wore. It was clear that he was not just a normal human person.

People would take Him in. He could give simple people enlightenment   something they would have never received in one lifetime, if they had not met Him.

Once you touch the light, the light will always be pulling you back to it.

Many of you have heard of a man named Braco, the person who just stars at people. I would really like him to say something important. So, in all the years he is out there he never speaks verbally to anyone publicly. I met him twice just to see him. He is just another person getting energy from people looking for a miracle to change their reality.

The more people follow someone the more energy they get. I am not saying its good energy even if it feels good. Ask a hunter that shoots his first deer, the adrenaline rush they get or the first time you have sex or the first time one gets high.

Soul and mind do not work together. They share our actions good and bad. It is ego that allows mind to think it is in full control.

Jesus was trying to teach His followers how to separate mind from soul. He taught listening to soul can be much easier than listening to the mind.

If you look at a computer it does what the programs are allowing it to do. A computer doesn't do other things until a virus gets into it. It then takes on a mind of its own and not in a safe way.

Soul is under the control of the body-home it lives in. Anyone can believe anything they want. It still doesn't make it true.

Jesus had the ability to touch a person and allow them to step out of their body in soul form. Many people including so called spiritualist spend their whole life trying to do that and never really reach it.

Now the truth about angels comes into play. Jesus never said He was an angel. They do not take physical bodies. Unless you watch a movie like Dogma or Constantine.

In our present reality, aliens have enjoyed more time in the physical realm then humans do now. If anyone's story had any proof that would be amazing. How come most alien races prefer the physical realm? I would say attachment to sex and food not God.

I was told by the Medicine woman I studied with. She told me she was allowed into a pyramid. She was one of a few people allowed in it. It was closed back up within days. There were two statues inside it. One was of Jesus and the other the Goddess Isis? Very few people know that or could see it.

Today woman carry a different energy, no matter what anyone says. They can hide from it but it will always be inside them.

Jesus never taught anything Moses taught. Moses was a man full of ego. Moses was the greatest Magician on this planet at that time. He had nothing to do with being spiritual. He truly cannot be explained in the Bible. He was not allowed into the promised land.

Man, created an idea about that. Most of his followers never knew what that was. Still today in man's thinking, the promise land is a place on planet earth. It was for Moses' followers.

They killed the people of a city they called the promise land, to take it over. They still believe it to this day that it is the promised land. God will never be in this realm and on this planet.

Jesus' parables never related to anything of earth. If you tear down my temple a hundred more will be here tomorrow. He never meant a real church. Jesus was not teaching about physical churches ever. It was man's limited understanding trying to understand what Jesus was speaking about. Jesus did not know mankind would except the negative teachers and teachings over His.

What one perceives as good does not make it good for everyone else!

Something Jesus really did not know was that people were going to be controlled by aliens as much as demons over His own words. When He came out of the dessert after being with a king demon, He now realized the dangers of this world for people.

How were People going to prove the difference between demons and aliens?

Are possessions and abductions going to be dealt with in the right way?  Man, always finds a way to humor himself and tries to protect his thinking or ego.

The newest word is Experiencer, meaning meeting with aliens in your room and having a great talk. While they have zero proof and say nothing important ever.

Jesus explained about the dangers of the astral plain and how it affects one when they are there. He explained about the time one will stay there and the karma one can work out there. Not all karma is worked out there. If you leave here with nothing you really don't have to worry about coming back except for people unless you are locked into attachment.

Jesus never really went into the Akashic records for many reasons. Man is still abusing the ability to read them if anyone really does.

Jesus told the disciples about the five lower worlds soul goes through to get to the true realm of soul. Some call it the soul plane or fifth realm. It is the last phase before one let's go of all ideas of anything relating to the body or form, to move into the formless you are now in spirit.

That is when one truly becomes light itself. It is not like all the lower realms. It now deals with the three rays of light, coming out of God. They flow through the five lower realms. You are now above any of the other beings, entities and life forms. One must be able to vibrate within the realm they are moving into before they are allowed in and able to stay there.

When you are in the highest of the lower realms, you are not thinking about how to feed the homeless or make married people stay together. It is not about building a bigger city or temple.

At that point, one becomes a true God to themselves, dwelling in one's own world.  You still will be under all God's true laws. Where that is, no one here knows. Would one take on a new body and start all over? No. You are moving into God realization. The souls that become totally awaken will understand God.

Jesus said to His followers never look back, do not do what you already know is wrong again. If God made one mistake, it would destroy all the universes and worlds that It took forever to create. God never made a mistake, I would say It always makes something better.

It is man that makes the mistakes and keeps making them. Jesus explained about us being soul not body. When He did many people did not understand. They just stopped following Jesus.

It is the same time when Jesus told the twelve main followers that they will all betray Him. One will do the opposite of what the rest are doing. That being what He needed accomplished. Few people will understand what Judas did was what he was asked to do.

Jesus never had to die. He had to if He wanted people to understand death and rebirth. Before Jesus, no one truly understood what death was.

Death was an idea the Egyptians' thought they understood. They did not. Nothing they did made it real to understand for no one came back and used the body they thought they could come back into. All the mummies were left in their little boxes to this day. The Egyptians starting to get a little closer to the truth and failed dramatically. They only had such a small part of the truth. Their understanding about death was so far off.

Reincarnation

Reincarnation is easy, not coming back is what is hard.

If you don't learn anything you keep reincarnating, why? When you reincarnate over and over how much do you think you really learn? When is enough -enough? Please think about that and then tell me one thing someone learned while staying here.

People feel they know what spirit is. Everyone has a different take on it. I listened to the best and they are the best at telling story and filling people with false truths.

Tell me one thing that Jesus taught that was a lie? Moses on the other hand kept adding to his list of stories.

When Jesus was trying to teach about the soul He related the physical body to the blood flowing through it. When He said, drink-wine and eat of my body-bread it was a relationship to an image of His soul. His teachings about soul was never added to the Bible for many reasons. Man, barely understood the body never mind the soul inside it as being anything different.

The comparison was easy for a simple-minded person to understand. If you relate to something they think they know, then they will think they understand it. The mind only knows what it is programed to.

People do not live by the teachings of Jesus. If man did understand His teaching the earth population would be getting smaller not bigger. Souls that become aware don't take on the ego and programming, they don't have to come back to save mankind. If God wanted that don't you think It would have made that happen? Never mind happen a long time ago?

The idea of man doing God's work is totally crazy. Jesus was still teaching as the people around him were helping to set up having Him killed. It was not Judas that killed Jesus, it was many of His own followers. It comes to the point that people need to think they are important. They want to be right. It is easy to set someone up as the fall guy.

Unconditional Love again.

Many things Jesus said went unheard. When Jesus said don't be angry over another person, He meant if you don't have a cause. That part seems to be missing from many people's understanding. Love everyone with what unconditional love? I will repeat this; unconditional love is the opposite what people think it means. I am sure you don't understand that. When you say, you are supposed to love everything, that is a condition.

Is it easy to understand that nothing going into a person is evil, only what you allow to affect you and comes out of it?

Jesus was teaching many things. It is when it all truly started here on this planet. He allowed the truth to be known for it truly was not before.

Jesus spoke of the blind leading the blind. It is the way most everything is still today. Both will perish and start their karma all over again. They will not pass the astral plane. They will learn how easy reincarnation is.

In the Bible, the New testament Mathew, Mark, Luke and John are still speaking about Moses' teaching. They speak about cutting whatever appendage that does evil to cut it off. Jesus spoke on that. Saying Moses was not right.

As you become aware you know what to do and what not to do. One should listen to their true self or soul. Instead of rationalizing their actions to be pure.

There was a time in my life, I thought I was evil and decided to take my life. The same as if your eyes deceive you, pluck them out.

It is better to get into heaven than not, if you can get rid of what is wrong. I will tell you the mind can be quite deceitful. That was Moses teaching not Jesus's. Soul is never wrong when soul is an aware entity.

I was given many visions of life beyond the body. There are nine kingdoms of God. There are three in each. There is no use to talking about experiences after the fifth realm. You do not come back here.

Do you want to stay here? Why would you? To save all the ants crawling on the ground, all the maggots eating dead animals or the animals that eat every other animal?

We are all killing our body in some way. Either by food or drink. If one is not aware of that, they are not aware of air and water. Man's own actions are doing humans in, not aliens or demons.

If man understood one-word Jesus said, he would not be happy here. Jesus always spoke about the body dying, not living. At that time, one becomes a hand of God. In His teachings, He spoke about the soul not dying and that we live in Hell, they call earth. We grow when we learn to leave it for good. Jesus spoke about how He won't be here nor there. Meaning living on planet earth.

If one looks for the greener pasture here on earth - the saying the pasture is greener on the other side. It is true, when you speak about soul outside of the body. It will never be that in the body, never.

Without the experience of death or even an out of body experience, one can never truly know or even understand spirit or God.

Thinking you know God, is only "thinking" mind programs. With all the speakers, I listen to holy or not, did I ever hear anything important about an idea of what God truly is. All men have taken the idea of God being a loving compassionate being. That was not what Jesus allowed man to see.

The real actions of love Jesus showed with Mary M was never shown in the Bible. It was never even accepted. Many lies were feed to man to keep them from seeing the truth.

Because of the story of Adam and Eve, man, thinks man is the important one and woman will always be second in his mind. Even though that whole story is one lie after another. I will explain that later.

How many men understand love of a woman? They understand love of sports, drinking, partying and sex better than a woman. Jesus' disciples were married.

Jesus spoke about leaving your family and friends to follow Him. What did that really mean? Families are dead locked into wrong programmed ideas. If one would have stayed they would never touch the truth Jesus was showing them.

In Scientology, you are trapped into a programmed idea. You cannot escape. Few people do in an effective way.

I am speaking about the three-main religions on this planet (out of two-thousand) why is there no truth about God? Nothing can even relate to IT? I am sure people think God is all about God being forgiving, but for what, everything? Do you think Gods' laws care about what man thinks?  The Bible makes it sound like Jesus excepted what Moses was saying. Whoever wrote that had no clue of the truth. Jesus was not into mutilating things, especially one's self.

God is the creator or destroyer, not man. When man thinks that, they start trying to be what they don't know. What good do you think will come out of that, robots, droids or soulless beings? That is the opposite of what Jesus was teaching about death of the body and moving into ego.

Man, now has pills to do everything. Making them live longer, become smarter, grow bigger body parts, feel better and even to travel is some dimensional world. I am not speaking about LSD or MDA.

They are all the things to stay in a body that have nothing to do with being spiritual. The body never becomes spiritual. If you look at all the body actions, voluntary and involuntary actions we are all gross. Remember what Jesus said only that comes out of the body is bad. Man's ideas are of what? Is it creating perfect sex, perfect rocket ships, perfect families? What do you think Jesus was saying? Any of those things?

Jesus was never speaking about traveling into space, or trying to live to you are a one hundred and fifty or more, or having ten children. He never spoke about how angels ministered to him.

People saw different qualities in Him that they could not see in other people.

The Maters cannot agree themselves as to the facts about the Council of Nine (spiritual council).

Nine is a number so that a vote from a voting system cannot be equal. Even that shows that the laws are not in perfect balance nor are men and they will never be here on planet earth.

Man creates more and more things to keep their mind off God. Many people have no values at all except to make money. Do you think entertainment helps humans move forward? Does any sport help's man understand God? NO.   When they pray before a game or event there are usually two sides to that. You hear the saying "Be on the side that is winning". That alone shows man's ignorance of how special Jesus was.

Jesus did not come here to change the world. He came here to save a few people's souls. His saying, "he who have little faith follow me". He did not come to reprogram the people that already had a programed idea. That is almost impossible to do in one lifetime. Unless one is open to truth. That means not one's truth but God's.

Given a program, one will carry it out if possible. That is how the Governments gets someone to kill someone. Hitler was one of the greatest hypnotists on this planet, he controlled a country through it. That means doing things you know are wrong and against your own conscience. In doing that you lose your own truth. The Christians were great for doing that.

If Jesus healed you, it was for life, not like many of the psychics of today. He then said go out into the world and live a good life. Once you are given the truth you are singularly responsible for your actions with it. There is no turning back. You just cannot. In the physical body, the passions will haunt you. Every second they dwell in the mind.

Killing, rape and lying are serious problems that create so much karma. One cannot pay it back in a lifetime or even a few. The abuse today is still growing but so many people say the opposite is happening.

Jesus faced Lucifer here on this planet He did not have to go to another place called hell. Why would people think Lucifer would be there? He has many of his workers here as well, trying to give people his idea of truth and fill them with false truths or lies.

Once Jesus went through ascension He did not eat much ever again. He was already living on the light. Guided and moving by the sound current. I challenge anyone out there prove their light is one tenth as bright.

I am sure many people are truly ignorant of truth. They except what the people wrote in the Bible holding that as truth. When there is none.

Jesus came here for one reason and one reason only. It was about how to get the soul ready to leave the body and then how to get where you need to take your next step. What you really will do when your body dies.

Yes, a few masters taught about parts of the astral plane. I am not sure if anyone truly understood it at any great level. Why would you want to go there in the first place? Why some people stay there and most others must come back? Being there is not as important as people think. It does allow however, one to feel they are connected.

The Astral plane is only the first plane. It is where all souls go to or through. Most people cannot go to the next plane or realm.

Hell is not easy to leave.

Plane, realm or bardo is a world that has its own laws. It has its ruler or what I call little god to keep it in order. It is much more enforced then here. That is why one needs to learn a few things before they even get to stay there, or even go there.

When Jesus said in His Father's Mansion there are many rooms. Don't forget He was speaking to simple minded people. They knew very little about spirit.

I need to also explain something very important. Jesus never came from ego. People think they are important to everyone else living here now. They are not important to the people that moved on to the next realm.

In four-hundred-thousand years, how many teachers came and what did they teach? The greatest minds were few and not one other really spoke about a real God.

I don't agree with science, psychic doctors or any medical doctors. They all play in the game of life. Man's thinking is a sickness. What is it composed of is sick. It's mostly sex. I'm not saying that is wrong but it can be. Ego thinks everything it does is important like making a plane or a TV. Man is always bored and must keep creating new toys to play with.

When Jesus was tortured and killed it went on for many days. No man on this planet could endure what He did for that long. When He came back He found all his followers had let go of his teachings for they truly did not understand it until He did come back.

His teaching would have been completely lost had He not returned from the dead. Jesus always knew He had to die and come back.

All his traveling was truly unknown. He did go to the pyramids and learned all his gifts there. It was where He went through ascension. He recovered all the gifts that were given to us and were lost. That is when awareness, became important. Knowing what to do with it and the right way to go about using it.

Let's get into the heart of all Jesus' teachings.

How much is really in the Bible? Who really told the truth anytime in History? Before the Bible was the Emerald Tablets, Samarian tablets, the Urantia, then the Koran, and a few others. What is true in any of them? How much is alien's programs? How much was really blocked from us? When were they really written?

Now is the important part. What God or Gods were they speaking about?
The Koran, from the prophet Muhammad of Islam, Really? I mentioned that is the teachings of Gabriel. Who else in history did Gabriel teach?

Many people today say they speak to angels. Why don't they have any words to prove it or actual proof to back it up?

Out of all the prophets that came out in two hundred thousand years, how many brought something important to change the world?

Today there are two point two billion people now following the Christian religion and about one point nine billion people follow the Muslim religion. Many of the rest follow another five religions leaving about two thousand religions more. I will say only about four have any more truth then the rest about soul and God.

If any had any important truth you would think the world would be in a better place not a toxic war zone.

A person trying to translate words from another person is just like anyone trying to translate a poem. What did the writer really mean when he wrote it and why?

Now, we have greater story tellers then Moses, here preaching their twisted lies about aliens.

With all the teachers and prophets that have come out since the beginning of time, why is killing still excepted under any law? You cannot kill people in your own country but go to another country that we are fighting with and you can kill anyone there. If you kill woman and children it is justified.

Whose teachings are teaching the truth about Death? Not the ones that say you will come back as whatever you are thinking or want to. Not the ones that say you can come back into a physical body you had. Jesus did come back to His astral body not his physical body. He never said it was important to reincarnate, which it is not.

The word incarnate means being aware of your earlier or past lives when one returns to earth. A soul doesn't have to incarnate if one becomes spiritually aware. If one does, one will be aware to finish something otherwise they will be forced into returning to finish their karma. If your aware you can work out your karma here and now before you die.

Jesus spoke about the astral plane and everything above it, only to His disciples that understood death. He could speak to most people, for they barely understood a relationship. In those times, it was not very meaningful.

Woman were always simple slaves to men with any kind of power. In all our history, how many women were recognized as spiritual? The most famous was Joan of Arc. She was one of the few.

I ask you how can a religion come out with so many lies and still think it is important to the world? To put out a movie like Risen, which was one of the worst lies, when they expect it to be important is sad.

Jesus had the hardest time teaching the disciples what haven was, understanding His teachings and what they really meant. The teachings would give them the ability to understand soul and what that really meant.

Many of the other gospels that were not in the Bible give a little more understanding of what Jesus was really teaching. When you discuss more it becomes different, you have a few more pieces of the truth.

Without an understanding of soul, you will not understand anything Jesus said at any spiritual level. When It is brought down to the physical level, it has nothing to do with spirit. All life teachings, teach nothing about death. Why?

At least now most people will have a better insight of what the words I use really mean.

Father in Heaven, people think there is a father image in heaven with man's limited understanding of spirit and soul.

In the first thirty years AD, man was having a challenging time just to eat and take care of one's family. (Not that is much different today). Relationships have not grown stronger. Science is giving people their own take on spirit and what we are as humans.

Next, man created the concept of the Father. More importantly, shouldn't it be Mother? The female energy gives birth.

Today man still has a challenging time. Taking care of children is really a tough situation when there is no mother for the daughter. Man's sticks to the program. Man is the most important.

Man's life is still no different than two-hundred-thousand years ago. Sex and cheap thrills is all man needs. Most men relate love to sex and not the opposite. Love can become a part of sex and it might be there for a while, if that fades away usually the relationship ends in just sex. Sex could fade away and love could still be there.

Man's desire for change comes into play. He starts looking for different sex partner not love in most cases.

When Jesus was teaching how could you explain Love? You couldn't. You can only show it and experience.

If you doubt it, you need to read the Bible. Jesus said if you believe in the Father and Me you have everything given to you of the Father. That is the Bibles wording. Jesus said I give you the teachings to meet God.

The Father not being a Man or a woman was very hard to convey to the people. He had to create many scenarios, metaphors or parables relating to something one does know to something else one does not know.

Most people need a physical action to believe, to relate it to a non-physical thing.

Spirit is invisible or I should say not solid like a tree. Blood is the way all living things relate to all other living things that are solid and alive. When Jesus appeared to His followers He was not solid. He was not filled with blood. He was not skin and bone. They saw the actual light body.

Relating things to a God which most prophets could not, was a fact. They could not prove anything they said.

The abilities called psychic powers gave a person the title of being demon or devil. Later that became a witch.

Now, all the so-called beings that became a God to many people were super powered. In all the stories. They always were made out to be bigger, faster and stronger than anyone else.

The deities were not human looking in most cases. They had the ability to speak, give orders and create a certain kind of thinking in people. Most also dealt with sex in many ways.

Have you ever wondered why no Gods are manifesting here and now? When Jesus said my work here is done. It was a reality check for people. Even the angels stopped coming down for mankind.

Why are Christians waiting for Jesus to return? Would they not kill Him again? They did not except his teaching then. They said they did. One must look at their actions and listen to them speak.

Man, has given his truth of God over to his own ego. They think that it is right as well. No man will understand God until they first understand Soul. That means understanding thyself first and living by that. No karma can be taken away by anyone other than God's angels or deities. Jesus' teachings gave man a way to follow and live life while they are here.

If you read the story of Milarepa

(Tibet's patron saint) you will get a little more understanding of that. He was one of the most powerful magicians. He had to learn about using magic, which I did at sixteen.

It was about and still is about not creating more karma. Understanding how to work off karma that you have. No one goes past the astral plane until they do. Most souls will have to reincarnate, no matter what they think or think they can do.

Karma a word Jesus could not speak about to most of the people around Him. He used the word death and eternal life. They could see death at a physical level. The hardest part of Jesus' teaching was not doing the miracles. It was explaining life after death of the body and then what allows a soul to do that.

Those teachings were only breaking the ice for His followers. He had to teach the actual technique to leave the body. That is something Jesus absorbed when He went through ascension. Only a few souls ever did in all people's history. No matter what you hear, no one goes through that. Many say they do. Ascending into the astral world is not the same by any means.

There are few teachings about when one ascends. They come from a few things, a death, death experience or out of -body experience. Nothing you read or are told will make you understand that until you have that experience. You do need to have it.

Jesus started speaking about past lives for a very important reason. That is having karma you must come back to work off. It was not like He was going to take it all away. Jesus died to show and understand death, reincarnation, and the astral body. It was not taking everyone's karma away from them. I am trying to press that idea on you if you think different. You cannot get rid of your karma without doing the work.

Jesus' teachings involved knowing the truth. One needs to live by His teachings. Sin was a concept that was relating to karma. They were always the same.

When Jesus was doing healings, it was to help more people see the power of spirit.

Jesus said there will be one greater than He. No one can step in that spot to this day. I wonder why? Maybe because man is moving backwards. People are leading people away from the truth. With all the talk about how spiritual one thinks they are. With all the people claiming it, do you see anyone? Healing without being able to speak about God is Ego.

I am not talking about the common idea that God is love. Thinking you can control God, seriously? God does not need someone else to do Its work.

Something never spoken about by anyone today is dreams vs. visions. Have you ever felt complete love, happiness, compassion, pure bliss, incredible trust, complete honesty, boundless beauty and then see the light of a thousand suns, knowing it will never go away? Why not? Visions go beyond feelings in dreams. They also show you incredibly important things. They do merge with dreams at some point. That being the past and the present. It is up to you to create the future.

It is all the lies of life. To think, anything you have in this world is permanent and everlasting. Everything will be taken away from you. Your home, your children, your friends, your health, your strength, you mate, your pets, the ground you stand on, your breath and even the vision you hold, meaning your eye sight.

After you move into your new astral body your awareness will be greater. It all doesn't happen that way unless you become aware in this lifetime.

Many people dwell in illusion after illusion. They think one day it will stay. They think you are supposed to stay on planet earth forever.

Now, through the voice of Jesus, echo's the sounds of truth that says give up everything including thinking everything will be handed to you.

It will only become eternal and forever when you release the body not before. This would include releasing man made ideas, thoughts and programs.

Because you feel blood being pumped by the heart doesn't mean you are alive. When the heart no longer beats that is when soul is released.

I am not a Christian. That is a man-made word. Jesus was a man that happened to be truly in tune with God. His physical mother was Jewish. That doesn't mean His teachings were Jewish.

My connection to Jesus will truly never be matched. Never will there be an idea of permanence here for me. I still would give my life for Him in a second in this world and to my partner.

While being able to experience the highest love physically, most people have no idea to how to touch its core which connects it to being spiritual. Kundalini and Tantra sex don't even come close. Tantra is for a very brief time and only moves into the astral plane. Then it is taken away. All the true teachings one has learned will come into play. Hopefully, somewhere along the road, you will have learned something outside the program or what I call the box. Man's programmed ideas of his truth will shatter just like a mirror.

When man was killing Jesus, little did they know they were killing all the dreams of God for mankind. If anyone can say the simplest laws that were handed down to us were wrong, please look in the mirror and tell yourself why. Then tell me. Hawksblood1@aol.com

Moses, who received the greatest gifts abused them. All the teachers on this planet speak about physical laws not spiritual laws.

The people around Jesus were following man-made Gods before Jesus. Look to the past two-thousand years. What Deity or Gods do you see working with mankind?

Man, cannot fathom spiritual ideas, if you had to choose between your child and your mate and one would die who would you chose? There are three options. One, go down with them, two pick your mate or three pick your child. Which one would you choose? The one mankind conditioned you to.

The story in the Bible about doing whatever God told you to do, would you?

If anyone understood the stories Jesus told without their ego would be able to experience many greater things. Knowing your God, you would know what you are supposed to do.

Do you have the right to play God? Many people think they do.
That alone goes against the
Ten Commandments. That is ok because man thinks they are better than them.


I will rewrite them in full.
1. I am the lord thy God, have no other Gods before me.
1. It has nothing to do with all the little gods, aliens or demons. IT does not say create them whenever you want.
2. Have no carved images of that is in heaven or below the ocean.
A. How many people even have a clue to what a real God would look like? They come up with the saying God created man in Its' image. Man, recreated it to mean God was created in man's image. It's

nothing even close to a real God. We cannot even compare ourselves to a deity.

3. Never use God's name in vain.

 A. Most people do, How's that? If not, God they will use Jesus Christ even if they are not Christians, how's that? Why no Buddha, Ala, Mohammad, or any other name? One subconsciously uses the highest form then can think of?

4. Keep the Sabbath day holy.

   A. Do people know what holy means?

   B. Why was it one day? Most people could not donate one day never mind a whole week, a month or the rest of their life to something especially God.

5. Honor you mother and father. Is that the way the followers honored Jesus? Helping kill Him? Honor like respect needs to be earned.

   A. Parents need to honor their children as well.   Both need to earn respect to get it. It never should be just given.

6. Though shall not kill.

A. There is no given excuse, no reason ever. Man, is not a God. Moses was one of the first to go against Gods spiritual laws. The only law that could have changed the world instantly.

7. You shall not commit adultery.

It is one of the acts that cannot be forgiven. That means creating too much karma that one cannot pay back in a life time. It is in the Bible, and most people will never even read that. Jesus told His followers that truth, as well as the street people. I am not sure anyone heard Him. Now, they just pass over it.

8. You, shall not steal.

That goes with abuse. Taking something from someone else when it is not given. That means anything. Even love.

9. You shall not bring false witness against your neighbors.

Man, wants what everyone else has and more. One will lie and cheat to get it.

10. You shall not covet your neighbors' house, wife or animals or anything of theirs.

What are your values, are they yours or someone else's?

Jesus was giving truth to His followers who had very little if they had any at all.

What was people's attributes of God before Jesus starting teaching? What were people's teachings?

Moses' God and Jesus' God were not the same. The Bible makes it sound like they were the same. Try to realize who really is writing the Bible stories and from where did the final Bible really come from? That is another story and not a good one. I spoke about that already. Moses's God was a jealous one.

When Jesus spoke of other worlds the only thing most people could relate to was stars in the sky. They would have pieced that with other stories they heard as well.

When soul gets to the astral world one gets to see the first real step towards the higher worlds of God.

Jesus was speaking to the people about Gods' rooms, many times, He left it at that. They related to God as a Father figure and the realms or worlds just as rooms in a normal house and what they could fill them with. They could not understand the real difference between them.

## The Five Passions

Attachment will make it hard to break away from all the things you are still are attached to. People usually are attached and usually will have to reincarnate. They will, depending on their karma, reincarnate within five to ten years. Based on that karma they have will decide what kind of family they will have to come back to. If your attachment is strong to your family and your karma is just you will come back to your family.

It was not Jesus' plan to speak about reincarnating as it is thought of today. He was hoping people would be wanting to get closer to God and not stay in this world. He was trying to get them off the planet and out of the lower realms.

Soul is separate then the mind. Soul holds on to things of the mind for a long time. That is the place where the five passions of the mind affect what soul will do in the next reincarnation alone with their karma. Their attachment will create the final place they come back to better or worse. Soul tries to keep moving forward no matter how small that is.

Man's lust is always looking everywhere for mental and physical pleasures, never incorporating true love. What's even worse is using drugs and drinking to help create that. The physical body is not more important than any of the spiritual bodies. People may think it is.

Man's greed, thinking you will never have enough money, power or even sex. Wanting more then what other people have. You will do anything to get it. That includes selling yourself to the devil. That is so real. It is not like what people think. Lucifer was angel just like the others that were sent down because of the things they did. If you don't think God learned anything from that think again.

Anger and hate keep you from being able to control your feeling., it makes it possible for you to hurt others. You become forced to work with energy that stops you from connecting to God/spirit. The thoughts you have do not allow you to relate to your true, pure feelings which stop you from connecting to your spiritual growth.

When you move into anger you will never be able to see the light or hear the sound or both, which are God's only way of working with soul.

As Jesus said I am the light. Man's vanity, thinking they are all that. Man's wanting to make themselves look better doing anything to try and create that.

Ego is at the highest level it has ever been in our history. The ego energy one thinks they have helps create whatever they want. It all has nothing to do with anything spiritual. It pertains to only the physical. It can be taken into a deeper idea based on hypnosis.

Man allows their actions to be affected mentally by their idea of it.

With technology, things like implants, butt implants, breast implants and even changing body parts become real. Making yourself feel you are more important than everyone else. Always lying to yourself. Trying to take everyone else's possessions and even their own stories. Making yourself bigger than God. It is a very sick world.

Man's attachment, filling yourself with desire for things, like your car, your house, your children, your girlfriends, making them important without the sincere desire of understanding God first. Which will always be the highest truth when one is ready for it.

Very few souls will ever get there. Saying there is no good or bad, really? Terrible things do not need to exist. Many people stuck in negativity need to pull other people into their twisted ideas.  It can happen from family as well as friends. They call that free will.

When Jesus said leave you wife or husband and your children. He meant they were already programmed with the idea of a false God. That is one thing no one will speak about. They just don't know. They will never enter the real kingdom of God in this lifetime or even many more.

To move past the astral plane into the next pure world should be the highest goal one has, but is it?  The next step is getting into the mental plane or third world.

The five passions are really minds way of having fun. They have nothing to do with spiritualism or truth. It recreates the idea of love into something that doesn't hold the same energy. It is the opposite of what comes from soul.

Man's has its split levels of Lust -Love, Greed -Giving, Vanity -Compassion, Anger - Happiness
Attachment- Gratitude.

These are the emotions of mind that will keep many souls from becoming spiritual. They are things like sports and competition. Sex and love. Drugs and drinking. Money and power. Connection and compassion. This is how energy splits.

The opposites are called the virtues.

Compassion is giving when it comes from the heart. Giving without the idea something must be given back. Happiness is being able to smile and laugh from one's heart. Seeing someone else smiling makes you happy instead of angry.

Smiling is something very hard for me to do with the conditions of the world's children now. How man allows it to exist? How can you?

Does happiness come from an inside source or an outside source? Does it come from inner experiences, day dreaming, praying the right way, or is it coming from giving yourself a cheap trill?

Gratitude is always thanking God for what you have and not attacking God for all the things you don't have.

It is knowing God will protect your soul no matter how terrible things get around you. It is being able to give something back life. It is being able to give back to the real world not dream land.

Giving, meaning being able to give from your heart and not your mind. It doesn't just mean money, but things like truth, feelings, friendship or real companionship. Love is living life with an open heart. Something that you can keep but don't expect someone else to have to give it back. Knowing the dreadful things are there and not letting them destroy you, or being able to share the most sacred things with another.

Jesus showed love everywhere He went. The mistake people make about love is that love was different then now. What they limit it to and look for in it. It was based on control over a woman.

People look in all the wrong places and to the wrong relationships. Picking a mate because they are different, cool or exciting. Why not because they are spiritual? I am not speaking about religions telling one who they can or have to a marry.

Anything other than God will take you off your own spiritual growth and you will be pulled into staying in this world for many reincarnations.

Jesus said the earth worlds are not the God worlds. Giving up the mind is not easy. The programs keep people locked on earth. Whether you will ever be able to see the truth about the higher realms after the astral plane depends on how fast you decide to work out your karma.

With all the info about aliens and people telling super crazy stories trying to make people think the help we need will come from them is ridiculous. I am not saying aliens are not real but they really are not going to help us.

Many relationships are what we really don't need in our lives. Few see that the main idea of life is learning and understanding death.

Something Buddha started teaching was moving into the Astral world, then the bliss state. His experience was in the bliss state. A place one can go. You should not intend to stay there for a long time. You do have free will, you can move forward or not. If you decide to stay there you lose that.

Bad relationships only bring stagnation, destruction and pain instead of the opposite. I learned the hard way. Many people think they need to do it that way. God Realization is as easy or as hard as we make it. Man, always makes it harder.

You can search out the right kind of people at any time to bring into your life but usually you don't. There are few people ready to move into the higher realms and many more that don't want to. It's because their enjoyment from attachment and cheap thrills.

Look at what people call their truth. Most people will say the sky is blue and the sun is yellow. They will speak about the weather. They never use words of

God, never. Preachers say thank you God. What they are thanking God for is money. That's not what they should be doing it for.

What is important? World news? Not religion or spirituality? No, they say don't speak about it. They speak about sports. Why? There is nothing gained except money. If you are losing you are losing part of your ego. That is a good thing.

They say don't speak about Politics. What else is there to talk about, the space program or aliens?

Jesus always was always speaking about death. Funny you never hear that word mentioned in the Bible in most of His talks. To this day most people are afraid of death and that was the main thing Jesus was teaching all the time and then had to prove it. Fear of death is their fear of facing a true God. They fear if they did all the right things in life? How is it, people assume they must meet God when they die? They have no understanding of anything Jesus was teaching. They accept all the false teachings.

Before I go any further I want to tell you a few experiences I had along my path to find truth.

I was brought up protestant until I was fourteen. At that time, I was going through conformation. I then went into witchcraft searching for truth. I was already doing hypnosis dealing with things people called psychic abilities. Also, I worked with a top psychic inside the U.S. in the late sixties.

Many times, during my childhood, I always had feeling's that I was with Jesus as my brother. I never learned why until many years later. Meeting with Jesus, brought there by the master I was working with at that time. It was my first meeting with Jesus, in the mental body.

After I learned of my past lives I realized I was following the wrong path. It took me years and five near-death experiences to change it all. I was in a religion or path for twenty years. It was the only one out of many that had any truth about the realms or worlds of God.

Now a little more detailed understanding about my closeness to Jesus. I was not on the road with him much. In the end times of Jesus, I was very close to both Him and Mary. Being impressed two-thousand years later only proves to me how incredible He was to me then.

I could except everything Jesus was teaching easily. Jesus was an incredible person.

Seeing all my lives and why I am here in this lifetime put it all together for me. It was to truly understand real love. The love I saw when I was Jesus. How to see God. The title of my first book. If a teacher cannot teach you how to do that they are not a teacher. If anyone thinks they are close to that, being one with God or the universe prove it?  Prove it to yourself first.

If you start a true search for truth every step you take is like stepping on a giant egg. Knowing that when you get to the top it will explode. Creating a totally fresh look at everything you thought you knew.

Jesus always taught at many various levels depending on the crowd of people around Him and their level of awareness. I was lucky to hear the truth about His secret teaching which were never mentioned in the Bible. The people doing the translations did not want them out. Never mind they never got to listen to Jesus directly.

The important parts were how to understand God and what God created us for. Why He created earth as well as many other life forms, the different realms between them and the worlds the little Gods are on.

I will tell you man is the most aware race about a God than any other race that I ever heard mentioned. Even at that man is still actively creating his or her idea of what he wants God to be.

Aliens races show how much they know by their actions which is nothing except technology. Tesla was given technology but is it really going to help us?

Alien races are advanced in technology but spirituality is lacking. Look at any help they gave us or will give us anytime soon. Then look at our history.

Jesus tried to teach about living life and preparing for the future of a soul without the body. Allowing soul to take as long as it wants.

The difference in truth is when a race starts destroying anything God allowed and created.

The lower beings, the little Gods had the ability to change the world. That could bring the ending of a race or the biggest part of it. That is where the Council of Nine * steps in. If you want the truth that it is up to us.

Jesus never taught about committing suicide as a way out. Which I learned myself. We all pick a way to force certain things to happen. It is being created many ways in our life.

The firmament around the planet is what creates the time frame we live here in (one hundred and twenty-five years) which is what it is right now. Man is trying hard to change that.

Jesus taught His followers how to do a spiritual exercise. It would bring them into awareness but they had to worry. After they killed (crucified)* Jesus, people doing any form of spiritual exercise were killed if caught.

Man has a small part of it called meditation that is without the gate keeper.

Without awareness, you go nowhere. You do need to focus. It should be on whatever you think you are truly looking for, God or spirit.

The disciples that had learned what Jesus was teaching were few and did experience the higher worlds. In that place, souls want to stay. Just knowing you are there when you arrive is most important. Most people do not remember. People that had a death experience may not see all the truth about that they should.

It is like eating hot dogs and then getting served lobster and steak. It's like looking down a sewer or looking down a waterfall. There is no comparison. I have experienced all the lower and higher worlds. If you make it to the third world before you die you are given the greatest gift you can get on planet earth. Nothing can be better.

In the end times Jesus always had Mary M around Him. Without her, His followers would have never been able to teach and bring His message to the world. I am not speaking about our times now. Many of His students did not have to reincarnate again. So much of His teachings have disappeared and most of what we have today is corrupted.

Nothing from then on was ever mentioned. My last good bye was when Mary M had to go into hiding with Sarah. I am sure her story is more important than all the others in the Bible. Men will never except that.

The Nights of Templar were working for Mary's daughter many years later. I am sure Mary was not there when they built the four temples or pyramids before they were all ordered killed. Only a few survived to this day. All writings after that were lost because it was rewritten over again. If you did not know Jesus or Mary you did not know His true teachings.

Jesus was speaking about walking on the path of truth. Living in this world being aware of the higher realms always.

Buddha taught one should always be thinking about death every minute. I'm not sure why for he did reach the fourth plane only to go back to teaching mind stuff, without the idea of a God. Buddhists focus on deities or what I refer to as the little gods of the lower worlds. There are a few that are incredible to work with. Not all of them are.

Jesus was not accepted by many religious people until He healed them. Seeing is believing. The truth in that is that one just had to stare into His eyes to experience the connection to the light. I know the people that did were able to start to understand spirit. There was very little understanding of it before.

When Jesus spoke, who do you think was doing the writing? Out of all Jesus followers only two could even write. Which they did when they could, but only of what they could understand. That was not much until He returned. They had no truth, other than Jesus was a healer. Now they had a story to tell. Most of the Templar were killed off very fast. That is part of the secret teaching as described in the Emerald tablets.

The worst part of all this is that man did not understand what Jesus was teaching had nothing to do with living here on this planet in any fantastic way.

He said live by the laws and if they are wrong change them. We don't even do that now. How is that? He said give to God what It deserves. I don't see many people doing that today either.

Even our constitution was stolen from the Native People. Our own Government is making sure we cannot use it the way it was intended.

People wishing Jesus would return like people think Buddha will return, really?

Man is so desperate about getting help from everywhere other than where it really is. Inside oneself.

If you were to hear Jesus now do you think anyone would understand what He would be teaching? Would they except it? All the New agers speaking about becoming spiritual and raising their vibration, to what, Jesus' level? It's called Christ consciousness.  Really?

People like using words like Christ Consciences. To know that word, you would truly need to know Jesus and then be able to do what He did. There is no one on this planet that can. Jesus did say there would be souls like Him to come. They never came and man has decided to go backwards in their spiritual growth.

Now people are looking to aliens and angels for help. The whole idea about meeting with angels or guides is what many people use today as their saving grace.

Jesus went into great deeps about the demons. Man thinks if he likes what he sees it must be good. Angles only come with essential information. They are not like some TV person on the air every day just to entertain you. They don't come with trivial messages. They don't care about your sad story unless it pertains to the whole earth or people. Today demons are not even accepted as real unless it refers to one being crazy. I am sure many of the same people believe in angels or spiritual guides, unless one works as a psychiatrist. Then they must live within a programed idea of sanity.

If Jesus was here today people I don't want to think about how He would really be treated? Like a King? No, like a crazy demon or on drugs.

You might not agree but look at all the people saying they work with angels and then listen to what they say. Interesting, no one is speaking about a real God or even worse what would It be saying to us now. Man's ego would stop most from even listening.

Do people believe they are really doing God's work? That being? I am sure many think it is about saving the world, feeding the homeless and making love.

How about making the world a better place for our children? Are we cleaning our oceans and the air we breathe? Is that happening anywhere really? I do not see man doing things to make the world a better place compared to what they are doing to destroy it.

If God is not real to you there is nothing I could say that will make you believe in IT. God is something that no one teaches about to this day.

All religions had a starting point. Who is that person? Where did his truth come from, dreaming, daydreaming, visions or from where? Mohammad's came from an angel? Still, who understands God enough to speak about IT? Really?

Can one say they faced God? If you do guess what? Everything you knew prior to that becomes the lie. I had many problems in my life because of that. It only makes one true to one's self.

Most people cannot remember their past lives, which they have had many. There is also the sick idea people are programmed to have about being in Heaven. They believe they will be sitting around speaking to family members forever there. Which wife or husband and from which life time, what? Only your last one?

People don't become aware or become angels because their physical body has died either.

What one thinks is important here is not important in the next world. Many people have a false idea of that as well. Many religions have no idea of a different realm, except heaven. They even have less truth about what God is.

Man's only thought on God was It is man like. So, man created God in their image. That would-be man's way of thinking. Who suggested that their idea of God must think like us? That meaning love all life and that it is important.

If all the Priest and Rabbis would have listened to Jesus all things could have been better. In Man's world, nothing existed except the idea of power and control. Losing control would be dangerous to their ego. It was never about getting ready to move into the next realm.

There is so much of a difference from what Jesus taught and what people said He taught. All religions speak about Love. The Ten Commandments do not use that word in them. It doesn't even suggest love. Jesus teaching were written by man.

I will repeat this for it has the highest of His teachings. He traveled to a pyramid.

Not the way most people would think. That was at a different level.  There were only two ways He could have done that. One was in the physical and two was astral travel, which was the first step Jesus starting teaching. Now called astral projection not remote viewing. They are both real.

Astral travel is what one does when they start going to the astral plane. It is not ascension. It is so different because one is using the soul body. The higher body soul takes. I am not talking about ascending which the body goes through when souls leave their physical body to be in the astral plane.

I try to stay away from speaking about the two other dimensions of the physical worlds. That is where some souls get stuck or are forced to stay, which includes spirits, souls and entities.

Jesus was teaching about moving from this world to the next or further. Men were still holding on to the idea of heaven.

There are many interpretations of what Heaven is. It is where God dwells. Now what is heaven really? Please don't listen to the translations from the Bible written by men about what it is. How many people have really experienced it? Did you? Many of the stories are based on visions but with what or with whom? Did they even know one they were taught and believe it?

All the stories about what happens when you die are just that.

Unless you have experienced the astral plane, you have no clue to what it really is. Men that attempt to translate words out of the Bible are translating what someone else thought into what they think. Neither are right.

Religions speak about three heavens in translations. They consider the Sun and moon a heaven throughout history. It is not. They are all part of the physical world. It has nothing to do with heaven. Souls don't float around the moon or the sun when they die.

The second world, is not the stars. They are still part of the physical world. The physical body can't go there.

People have the ridiculous idea of the third world being where God is and where the angels and deities dwell.

The rooms/realms Jesus spoke about were different. They were for souls of different vibration. He sure was not talking about the bedroom or the kitchen.

There are the little Gods that dwell in the five lower words. There is a deity for each realm. If one thinks of the realms there are three parts that is the physical, astral and mental. There are nine others. They each have three parts to them. No one ever speaks about that. When you hear about the sixth dimension that is still in the physical reality.

After the fifth realm, you are only using the soul body. That is the last connection to all the lower worlds. You now are moving into the higher worlds of God that are allowing you to use ITs extraordinary gifts. Now you can create your own worlds. Now you feel you are one with God but you know you are not God. There is no ego. It is now you and what God allows you to create. Under all Gods laws which now are accepted by you. You become them. There is no other experience except what you create. You talk to yourself now.

Being outside the body a death experience usually only touches the astral plane. Unless you work with high angels and deities you will never get past the astral plane. I am not saying everyone that does remembers much or any of it. The Human mind can only fit things into what it can perceive. Until you let go of mind, soul can never be its' true self.

I am not speaking about the religion of Jesus which is man-made. He is the only one I have ever met teaching the true teachings as I know them. His teaching was not just about healing the astral body or falling in love here.

In the physical world, there are so many things to learn about living here. As you move into higher realms each realm becomes more spiritual. One living in the physical world without any experience of the next two realms have no true understanding of God's world and truly doesn't understand his mission here.

People that studied with Jesus were gifted, just to be able to look in Jesus' eyes. Eye to eye is a connection to soul itself. Any person that saw Jesus walking or speaking could feel His aura and that alone would change one's energy.

To have real true Darshan was and is incredible lucky. There were not that many souls able to experience that. It is still possible to have it today. I don't hear anyone really speaking about that the way it should be.

Saying you see God, one would have to prove to themselves. If you express it to others, you must have complete confidence in your vision. One becomes the carrier of the light here. There are various teachers speaking about receiving that while they have no real clue or a true connection to GOD.

You can tell by their words. All the so-called teachers that walked this planet never speak about a real God.

After my whole life of experiences and awareness of my past lives, I see the truth behind all things that Jesus taught me two-thousand years ago.

You can break down all the lies from any speaker when you ask yourself why? Why love? Why peace? They don't exist on planet earth any more as morals do not. That should really make you wonder where man is really going and were we really are? How about nowhere good.

I will ask you what do you know about the Ark of the Covenant? Why was it so important?

Why, do you think no one is really trying to prove it exists? There are a few people saying they have it. They also say the Government has it. If that was the case, why do you think they will not show it to the public? Do you think they would use the ark? They cannot.

The Ark is a wood frame covered with Gold. There were two wooden ones, made as well. Which did not have the same power. They found they could not carry the real Ark into battle. It was too heavy. If you want to know what happened when it was brought into battle. Both sides suffered many died from it. They will never mention that in any Bible story.

There is no one that can prove anything about it really except the delusional people claiming they have it. It has The Ten Commandments in it as well as Jesus' blood which was placed inside later. If it was to be released to the world, I am not sure what would really happen. How many people would really be affected? People don't want to understand many things that happened have nothing to do with being in one religion.

The Ten Commandments were the only true physical laws of this planet that the little Gods allowed us to have.

Moses went against them in so many ways including killing, he was not allowed into the promised land from that act alone. The promised land being the astral plane. Everyone goes into the astral plane and only a few souls go through it to the third world.

Moses did go to the astral plane, he forced his laws of his sick mind on people. He truly never understood God's words. He also did not listen. He was a madman.

I have repeated that the words Jesus spoke were changed by the first person trying to re-write them. They were changed many times. They no longer have any connection to the truth.

In the King James version, Jesus spoke about Moses laws as if they were right in a few statements, (Which had to be placed there by someone else). Jesus was against everything Moses wrote and said.

Jesus never spoke about destroying the body. It was about healing the body and mind while here. It was not about killing, pain and suffering. Truth and compassion was most important.

Jesus taught different things to the common people then to His disciples. He had to give each of His true disciple's specific parts of His teachings. He could only give them what they could understand. Each received some of His psychic abilities accept Mary M. she was given infinitely more.

## Healing

Jesus spoke about healing people for a reason. It was not just so they could live longer. It was about learning to work through the karma they had to repay. He did not take it away. People cannot wish it away or just give it away. No alien race can take it away either. I am sure with all the false truths people are saying people really think they can.

There are two reasons.

1. So a person could work out their karma before they died. He did not just take it away. They did not have to take it with them.

2. A person had to learn how to connect with spirit then listen to it.

Today, how many people say they speak to God and then come out preaching love? That is not part of the Ten

Commandments or the teaching of Jesus or God.

How many people say they work with the high angels? Many use the angels in the Bible. They only work within the lower three worlds with the Three Gods there. That does include Lucifer. He is an angle as well as Saint Michael, Gabriel and the other seven all that fell.

Fighting in the other realms below the fifth realm still is not accepted. Many of the Deities did the same thing. It was right to them. Souls cannot be killed by angels or deities, really?

Jesus spoke about killing and a few other things in detail saying if you kill someone (intentionally) you cannot get into the higher words, period. That included things that were in the Ten Commandments as well. There is no atonement for that in one lifetime. Even if one dis-owns them. No healer or psychic can change that either.

People don't know how much karma the trivial things they do can create. One thing I will repeat is using Gods' name in vain. Rather than accepting their own blame.

Jesus went into teaching about what to do in time of trouble. It is not what most people do.

The statement if one picks up a gun they will die by it, is so true. Even if it is not an actual gun. That act changes everything you worked so hard to get to before that. That is only one way of creating karma. The same as Jesus said turn your cheek.

Soul is accountable for every thought that one allows to become a part of one's reality. Many things include lying, saying I love you without the responsibility that comes with it good or bad.

People have this sick idea it is better to kill your attacker then be killed. Why? Ego is man's sick thinking. Karma created in one lifetime can give you many more reincarnations to pay just one of those acts off. I do not have to say all the things that you know hurt your spiritual growth, right?

The worst thing to me is sexual abuse. That can be translated into many different things and ways of happening. Karma is not something that just disappears or is just forgiven. I look at it worse than killing.

So-called healers telling people they have healed in the name of God or their higher power. Do they have a clue into any person's karma? It boggles my mind how these people convince others that they will clear their karma.

Jesus cleared a few people's karma because God allowed Him to. He was the only one ever to be able to prove it. Jesus took His disciples karma onto Himself for what they did in His name. People think it meant that Jesus was taking responsibility for everyone and for whatever they did.

Excluding everything Judas did and had to do. He was one of the two closest disciples to Jesus.

When one uses God in their work they better Know IT and what IT desires.

Man is the one trying to brainwash people into thinking they can make this world better in some way. It is up to each soul to come to their own truth. Not that they must change anyone other than themselves. They just might not ever understand that. They will reincarnate so many times from that.

Man's thinking still doesn't have a clue of What and Who God is really. It is not the story book idea. It is not the programmed idea of the totality of Love.

If it was just that the world would be just that. We are the accumulation of all the teaching of deities and aliens now.

We were not that when we were first brought here. We were aware as Atlanteans living in harmony. Man has no idea of all the life that has lived here in the past five billion years.

We are supposed to accept a person like president Crump? Does he have any truth why humans are here and what spirituality is supposed to mean to us, and what we are supposed to do?

Scientists are trying to get us to believe what they think is important. I can assure you it is not spiritual. It is not about going to other planets or reaching the heavens like the story of the Tower of Babel. Trying to get to God in every way except the right way.

People make up innovative ways all the time. Their own actions show how much they are not really learning. How about anything? How about nothing! Then they must revert to science. Like science really wants to know a God. They create their own idea of God every day.

When doing your spiritual work use the word spiritual because now you are thinking about things outside the physical or what I call the box. When Jesus spoke about traveling the inner worlds, we were people that still could not travel other than by animals. There were only a few who could do astral travel.

They did see things in the sky. Their idea of flying was from birds. When it came to angels the idea about them traveling became an idea they had to have some form of wings. Wrong.

When they saw UFO's or meteorites they would relate that to things that they did understand like flaming chariots not ships. To this day people relate things to what they know, not what they don't know

In a dream or daydreaming, even in a near death experience one usually sees themselves with wings when flying. How long would it take an angel to get here with a pair of wings?

Even superman had to be created by man's idea. He used a cape to fly. Man's ideas changed from flying to flying carpets. Man's visions and experiences are usual controlled by the minds own awareness or lack of it, usually of the ideas what it was programmed with.

In an out of body and near-death experiences the mind can only translate what it sees into something it can understand. They are usually things of the physical mind. Only when soul is in control over mind can that change.

Why I am speaking about that? We all need to understand things we don't understand with souls' awareness and not mind's awareness which is filled with programming. Minds knowledge is mostly words of someone else, not actual experience or thoughts implanted by books.

The next thing is size. We think aliens and all creatures must be a certain size, from an ant to a whale. That is only because of minds programmed thinking.

Man assumes size is based on our idea of size itself. Can man fathom a two-hundred- foot man? How about an entity, one-thousand feet tall?

An angel can be any size they want. Would you except that? What if an alien race is the size of an ant? The things they do are the same or even much greater than a person. If they are giants they could be many times stronger. It's funny how an ant being smaller is ten times stronger.

Jesus did not go on and on about angels. He knew many fell from a higher level and were now locked in the astral realm. The higher beings were never mentioned in the Bible. I am not sure about the name Metatron a weird name for Bible time. Could it be an alien?

What, is and what was the alien's agenda? Mankind has been programmed by only a few things. One is all the carved tablets and writings left for man to read.

At that who wrote them? A spiritual being? A drunk. An alien? Today in the U.S. you cannot say things like I spoke to an alien or demon, you would be considered crazy.

The Emerald tablets are considered the oldest written words on the planet. Does that make them important? Who or what spoke to the people writing them? Gods or aliens? It is easy, look at the words used. The words don't go high into the higher worlds of God. I am not speaking about universes.

I want to speak about two separates times that were important to the planet. They are Atlantis and the time of Jesus' birth. Both were the fountain heads of truth and awareness for man. Atlantis being the time the world existed without killing and everyone had psychic abilities.

What if people today had to cut their tongue out?  What about one's mind if they are evil? That would go against everything Jesus was really teaching.

Seriously these things are in the Bible. I cannot say who rewrote what Jesus said. I would go back to the idea that only two of the four Gospels were of Jesus' twelve disciples. The other two were evangelists. Interesting how one was spending their time with Peter and one with Paul.

They were each given a chapter in the Bible. How's that? I really want you to think about what I said even if you don't read the Bible. How can two different writers write the same thing word for word? They cannot unless they were copying it, that would mean they did not experience it or even hear it from Jesus.

When Jesus spoke about the room's in His father's mansion, no matter how you interpret that, it meant something different then how man speaks about that now. They never tell the truth about what level the realm is at. They call it all heaven.

How about the truth. Every soul is going through a learning process. I am sure most people have no idea to what that really relates to. If you think it is about loving each other and living in peace, what animal lives in peace? What insect lives in peace? What fish lives in peace? Once upon a time whales had nothing to worry about. They are now dying by the hundreds every month. Man has no clue!

Even the few creatures that had no known enemies like the sea turtle and dolphins, now have man as an enemy.

If you look at men around the world they will eat every creature. Even Moses tried to make that wrong. He tried limiting what people could eat.

When Jesus said leave your family and friends do people understand why? Most important was being aware of your spiritual growth. Many things Jesus taught to the people were not understood. So how do you think man related to the secret teachings? It did relate to death, killing and understanding God.

In comparison, it is like trying to teach a child in kindergarten Einstein's theory, even at that he was wrong about many things.

If you want the truth you must dig a little deeper than your feelings. Do you know how many terrible things including killing came from one's feelings? It's the same for humans as it for animals. That is called surviving, a natural emotion of the body without thinking from any spiritual level. An aware soul can go beyond that.

Experiments like having a woman and a baby in the dessert with no food. How many woman, will do the same thing? Most, will do one thing, only a few will do something different.

In the animal kingdom, the weak usually get killed.

In a story of a plane crash, they had to eat the dead to survive. People should look at the way we live, thinking many things are ok or right. That is one of the reason soul gets stuck here over and over. Man ignores laws and so they despise the truth.

If one could hear Jesus speak now they might be able to understand what He was really saying. When He said over and over I speak unto you and you still don't listen, why do you think He would keep repeating? Man will go over and over something until he thinks he understands it and that will be his own programming. Do you know how to go beyond the human thinking?

I am lucky to know what Jesus was really teaching or taught. Mainly because of being around Him when he gave the most important message to His disciples and then the world.

- Out of all the greatest speakers now, I do mean the greatest speakers alive today, I haven't heard one talking about a real God. They have even less understanding of Jesus' true teachings and must relate that to the only idea people have that everything is all about love. Does that help people understand why they are here?

- If you don't think if God wanted a world of love, it would be that. If you don't think God could make it that way? Well IT did. Then you truly don't understand a real God. IT allowed man to destroy it as well. God only wants enlightened souls coming into the higher worlds or realms. That is for certain. Which Jesus called them rooms to the simple-minded people.

The whole idea that Jesus came back into a human body is one of the biggest lies in the Bible. When you let go of the body you are anything other than a body. You then need to realize everything that you think is important is not.

Your birth mother, which one in this life time or the earlier ones? Your children in which lifetime? Hopefully they all grew in awareness each lifetime their souls come back to earth. Do you think they think about one parent from one life time if they did not grow spiritually? Many accepting the programmed ideas which they will live with.

If you are ready to listen to what Jesus was teaching it was nothing to do with forgiveness. It was not human forgiveness He spoke about. It was not forgiving others. If you heard one-word Jesus said about death and giving your life to God, you might start to understand something about God, something else about what IT's true teaching is. It is all about one soul, yours (individually).

Thinking man is important why? Really for who? Their family? The job that they do? Not all jobs are even good or helping mankind move forward. Healers think they do such a wonderful job. Really? Is it for God, people or their ego?

When Jesus spoke about death and giving up the body it was the most important thing about soul's journey. The soul has a demanding time understanding the mind that controls the body. If you watched the matrix, please watch it again and think about being inside all the things described in it. Mind programming.

If you were to stay in first grade do you think things would change? How much? What if you were stuck in eighth grade? Do you think things would change much? There's people in collage do things really change? Is it for the better? As man grows in intelligence what is growing spiritually? Nothing. Ego grows with money and power but not the connection to spirit.

Jesus taught about giving to this world what is deserves, and give to God what IT deserves. Does anyone know what that is? It sure is not just saying you are one with IT. How can you be one with what you don't even know? How can you act like IT if you don't know how IT acts or what IT is or what it even thinks?

God created all forms of life from an ant to a dog. If you are aware you know ninety-nine percent of all dogs came from a wolf.

When God created humans, IT did have a mold. One that fits all that we are and have been. We all need to eat, drink, breath air, go to the bathroom, and yes die. All those things relate to the physical world or realm only. Do you think any of those things affect Ghosts or spirits? No, but ego and programmed ideas do.

Something to think about if you believe in evolution. Why would most things evolve and some would not? The roach is over two-hundred and eighty million years old and still very much the same.

Jesus Himself never said one will become God. One time someone wrote, He said, "My father and I are one". But He did not mean it the way the Christians interpreted it. God realization means you start to think as a God. You do not think from the mind but from soul. Jesus in his dying breath was still learning to understanding God, Himself.

When He said sitting on the right side of God he meant it that way. Not sitting on a thrown giving the orders. One becomes a creator in a way God allows one to.

What is wrong with the world today is that there are no spiritual beings here in a physical form. There is usually a soul holding the highest energy that no other can at any given time. There must be one.

Well he or she must be in hiding. While at the same time many others have come out saying they are that. Jesus thought there would be many after Him. No one could take that place today. No one.

I realized the idea of spiritual is not here now. It is not the Pope, the Dalai Lama, not Deepak Chopra, not Eckhart Tolle, not any of the highest paid speakers, not one religious person, are really spiritualist.

Now ask yourself why not? Not one of them truly understands God or the reason for earth and the physical realm being created. They add their two cents to say what they think about spirit. They don't ever speak about God. So why I am writing this book about Jesus is because He was the only one able to speak about God. There are a few that say they spoke to the devil. Really? Prove that one too.

To make it easier for you, imagine a world with all love, light and compassionate beings. What do you think they would be doing daily? What would they be speaking about? What do they like to eat?

What would you eat if you did not have to care what it would do to the body? Making what kind of things for what? Having children for what reason? One's pleasure. Take sex out of the picture what would man live for? Take children out of the picture what would a family be? Take the idea of excitement. Where would it come from? We should eliminate all sports for money. The human body is limited for a reason. Only when one can understand soul will they ever be ready to let go of the programmed ideas of death.

When Jesus taught, it was never about having an untroubled home and family. Moses on the other hand wanted the perfect home and complete control over it for the male. His sick ideas were his blame because of his own thinking not Gods. You must understand what God, Moses was working with. The saying "I Am all that I AM"?

Jesus died to prove His own teachings. Soul doesn't die. He had to show to all His followers to see it to understand it.

Do you know in the inner worlds that Jesus teaches about each realm or room within it? He named the Gods of each. There had to be an over seer of each realm. He called them the little Gods man calls them deities.

Without that there would be complete chaos. The worlds would be destroyed one by one if it was left up to humans, aliens, demons or even the angels. That is why God keeps the angels and demons below the third realm.

If one soul thinks they are God, they cannot move forward. There is a certain accepted level of thinking and awareness that is needed for you to be there and do anything.

The physical world is so corrupted. It seems to be getting worse while people say the opposite.

I hope you will see everything I am speaking about fits together with everything Jesus really taught. After spending years traveling the inner worlds you will start learning truth.

Jesus' touch could cast one in or out of any state they were in depending on their karma. Meaning into the next realms or world.

Let's talk about something no one ever speaks about. I mentioned this before about how two different gospels chapters are the same. Which is the story of Jesus with Lucifer. How's That?

It is not possible for two different writers to write the same thing. The same as the story of Noah's ark is twisted. There are words the Bible used -clean and un-clean. What is a clean soul and what is not? Whose story do you think you will believe? In the Bible, it says what sins are unforgivable. There are three mentioned. Find them if you even care.

What I really want to speak about is the time Jesus spent with Lucifer. The statement made was for forty days and forty nights.

Imagine being the most powerful or spiritual person on the planet. You had to stay in the wilderness with the most powerful demons that God allowed into the lower worlds. Man, is great for saying the good will win in the end. That is close to the truth.

In a timeless realm how long do you think that would really be?
Do you really think anyone at that time could understand timeless? Not one hour not one day but thousands of years. The words reincarnation and soul travel were unknown and never spoke about.

Do you think they could understand any of that? The darkness, the temptation, never mind not having food and water. Lucifer was tempting Jesus every single minute of every single day.

Soul when it becomes aware, is responsible as well as powerful. Now power is not under the control of ego. If it were God would not grant you it.

There are a few truths one can take out of that. That no matter how much power you have it is not the answer to truth. Thinking you can give anything other then what is needed of you and still be able to face God is a delusion. Bargaining will not get you there either. There is a reason for everything in life as well as death. It is called soul awareness. It is the hardest path to take.

Jesus spoke about souls losing their life while others will have eternal life. Do people really understand that? I am sure they don't. Dying doesn't make you an angel or anything more than a soul. Thinking you become a spiritual being is a dream. Nothing is just handed to anyone no matter how much money or things one has. You don't really have a place to go in the astral plane. You may think so. If a soul has any understanding of God and spirit, they would not have to stay here. What do people think their mission in heaven would be? Protecting souls here?

You can only move forward when you deserve it, so the idea of healing the world could never happen. Cloning would also go against all spiritual truths.

Back to Jesus facing the Darkness, Why, do you think that no angel could defeat Lucifer? Why do you think Jesus did not destroy Lucifer? He truly had the power over the astral world. Only in the physical and astral worlds does evil, negativity and sickness exists.

When Jesus started teaching He was no longer living inside the physical reality. He moved into the third realm to dwell. That is why Jesus spoke about many realms of God and earth only being the first.

People cannot deal with the concept of Hell. Think about it. Man's understanding is it is a place that you will go forever, if your bad. How about it is a place one needs to learn to get out of forever.

Jesus spoke about the higher realms to the ones that could understand it. The same as I am telling you right now. Will you hear anything I say?

On a box in the street, in some hotel hall, theater or church there is a person trying to tell you how spiritual you are and how protected you are.

There are woman and children being abused. They live in a world of being slaves to their masters. In truth, it could even be their husbands, father, brother or even their children. Man is that for sure. I am not saying it is right for it is defiantly not.

When Jesus said follow me He meant in an important way. In the Bible, all the statements from God were anything but from the story of Adam and Eve to even the story about Moses. It is about a third of the Bible. He never said He was God, did He? History is the greatest lie ever told. What kind of Gods were the first peoples following?

Could they have been following aliens? I am speaking about Adam and Eve. God or aliens used the words "OUR KIND". What kind is that, kind of a God? Read the story a few times it is only a few pages long.

In my viewpoint, the story of Adam and Eve was the reason of man's belief thinking he is better than woman.

Why do you think the Ten Commandments were important and still should be but are not? When they were written, they were considered the most powerful words on earth. They will stay in the Ark of the Covenant.

No man has the right to kill another. No alien does either.

As we get closer to a very serious time in the earth's history something incredible will be happening. Every race wants to reincarnate here now as well.

I did believe that in this life time, physical love was the most important. What I did find is that physical love is not even close to understanding God's greatness and truth.

When your body parts are gone your idea of love will change completely. That is after one leaves the Astral plane into the higher realms.

I did learn the reason why I chose to come back here to work something out. Soul must learn many things based on how much one did or did not learn already. I will say that it gives me all the reasons to move on and not come back.

Karma is always part of life here. If you don't know about karma or understand it. Without clearing your karma, you will have to reincarnate again.

Any religion that thinks things of the physical world are important to GOD, truly have no understanding of God Itself.

Why would God allow children in one place to live and children somewhere else to die? The lower angels and deities can help you go to the places you need to see if you are even ready for that. You can sit back and wait for aliens to come rescue you.

When Jesus spoke about man's forgiveness verses spirit's forgiveness they were two separate things. Meaning if you live on earth you can believe you are forgiven for whatever you do. You need to realize you are still controlled by mind and ego.

When you die those two things do not need to go along with you if you decide to let go of them. You now must deal with the truth with what you know about spirit and God. Suddenly all the things you do not know are not there to help you. The things you accepted and were told are not important will be facing you. Such as why you came to planet earth. Where you came from before that and how spiritual you are.

Dealing with things on the astral is different from dealing with them on the physical. For most people, it will be only a temporary retreat to think a little harder about what is real and what is not. Looking beyond the hologram which you are told life is.

When Jesus spoke about Jonna and the whale, it was a real story. He spoke about paying your karma.
A very important thing I need to speak about is going past the astral plane. There are no effortless ways of carrying that out.

All the lies and beliefs you have, need to be removed from your thinking. All the ideas that are fed to you about God and love. It's not close to what they really mean.

There is the importance of knowing where truth comes from. You don't create it. You need to experience where it comes from. Thinking you can truly experience it in the physical body is another fantasy.

Jesus worked with His followers at the level they could go or were at. Most could not go very far. Meaning the most important part was being able to leave their bodies. Learning to travel as soul. Jesus did not call it what man calls it today.

Life is about understanding soul not the physical body. Man has that backwards. Animals need nothing other than food. That is how man thinks except he wants lots of toys to play with.

Now that man can pretend he is God or at least one with IT, in his mind, he thinks he has the right to do whatever he wants. That means creating stories that have no truth in them. They allow ego to be in power creating one's story.

Astral plane is not home

The astral plane is the first stop for all souls. People call it many things from a bardo to heaven. It is not heaven. It is like driving up to a gate that blocks a road that leads to a giant mansion. You cannot see much with all the trees, plants and the fence in your way. You can hear beautiful music coming from it. Even if you could go past the gate, the car you are driving could not make it over the road to get to the mansion because it is like a mote with a drawbridge. If you think you can swim across the mote there are alligators in it. When you get to the castle you can see it is made from some form of gold including the big door.

You still insist on driving around in your car to find another place to go. You are holding on to the car like you are holding on to your body here now. I never wanted to work on cars nor do I now. I give the word Car-ma to Karma.

When one experiences that heaven is a man-made word or a dream you just might start trying to stop dreaming and find what the real world is. You are now in an incredible place of seeing things way beyond just your imagination to the way it truly is.

People that have their first out of body experience see things totally different now and from then on. Faith and belief only go so far, without experience, it is nothing. You can believe you are going to grow wings and fly all your life but in the end, all that time was wasted on the wrong thing.

If you had a hundred dreams of flying it has nothing to do with the physical body that you are living in. I guess that is why a plane is so important to people feeling that sincere desire to fly. It is not about where you are going. The most important thing is how you are going to get there.

It's your desire to see other things even if it is only for a week or two. In hopes that you will see differently. Well you just might see poverty. Most of the planet are in tough times, starving and even homeless. What do you really want to see a spiritual being?

When you die and you are looking at yourself as soul, you should think what happens next, while you are still alive.

You have faith and trust in your beliefs but what really happens? I already mentioned your karma precedes you. It has already decided where you will be in the astral plane and for how long.

I want to mention the things that keep you from staying in the astral plane or moving past it.  All souls vibrate at their own frequency just like every cell phone has its own frequencies now. Each soul has its own identity.

Five words, Lust, Greed, Anger, Vanity and Attachment. The root of these evils, all goes back to attachment. That can be anything from a car, a pet, drugs, family, sex, drinking or a place. Somethings you think are important to hold on to in any way you can.

Creativity is a very dangerous word. If you think God creates garbage you really need to think again. It is man that does that.

Why do people think they will be with their family in heaven? Is it something one heard from other people, a psychic or even something they read? To understand past lives if one did not have the experience, it will be impossible. What is not accepted is an idea of living with other families before the family you are with now. That would mean you could have been married a hundred times. You are not always the same sex either. Hopefully you will see the truth in this and then when you move into the experience, you will know the truth.

Most people assume that when they go to heaven, they will be with their present family, why? What if you were married three times in this life. Which wife will you be with? The one you left? The one that just died or the one you are with now? What if you were not married and went with a hundred woman, would you expect to be any of them?

In the Muslim religion, they believe when they go to their idea of heaven, they will meet many virgins that will take care of them. It says big breasted woman and all so says they will be hard for a very long time.

I would love to ask them will they believe that they can take care of them as well? They cannot fulfill one woman in this world. If that was even possible. They believe they will stay hard for ever. What a sick twisted idea of heaven. Why a woman would even be with a man like that is even sicker.

The old timers were loyal to the person they married. Hopefully that person was loyal to them back.

Do you think that your late husband or wife is sitting, waiting in heaven for you to finish working out your earthly karma?

I've said it twice already, no one becomes an angel just because they died. Few souls have the capability to go past the astral plane just because they want to. They must come back to work out their karma.

You can believe whatever you want. Without your own proof do you know where you really are going to be when your body dies? Can you except someone's idea?

Jesus spoke about the realms like a school. Starting with grade school, you start in kindergarten and you work your way up to the eighth grade. How much more did you learn? I am sure much of what society wants you to know but nothing about what God wants you to know. How's that? Do you learn one thing spiritual?

When you are learning how to count, add, and spell you lack any knowledge about God, spirit, the inner worlds and even alien races. You may be fed stories about religion, the Bible and faith, but really, where does that all get you? In high school, you get more programs.

A few religions believe you must give the Gods something when you get to heaven. They mix heaven with physical reality rather than the spiritual reality. That meaning things of the physical, solid world instead of the world of light, the light body.

If you really don't think I am telling the truth, check out young children that say they know their past life. They will start opening doors for all the religionists that don't believe in reincarnation.

I also think in a brief time you will understand that God did not just make planet earth for you to stay on it.

When people start being shown a little more truth what do you think they will do with it? Just as when Jesus was teaching his students, many went against Him. Ego always seems to get worse when power or money comes into the picture.

The word which is over abused by so many people again is ascension. Very few people will ever understand it or go through it. Dying is not ascension. It is called ascending. Ascending is dying and going to the astral plane. It has nothing to do with spiritual awareness.

I do not want to go against everything you think you know but what God did Jesus work with? It was not Jehovah or Bramham Gods on the third word. There are two other Gods on the astral plane, Braham and Cal-Braham. Let's not forget Lucifer.

All sounds vibrate out of God. All light comes out of it as well. The deities work with the lower five worlds only. Still they cannot make any soul become God-realized. They can only help you move on to a higher realm.

The Hindu people pray to two Gods. They also work with many of the deities in the next two realms. They do understand a little more about reincarnation and karma. They create more karma then needed by their own faith. Dealing with the little Gods or deities how many people ever meet with one or had a real conversation with one?

If I try to go into my version of what is right and what is wrong, you will run away. Anything that sounds like preaching is not excepted by most people unless they are Christian. I cannot name another other than Jesus that had something to say and could change the world.

The council of nine from Atlantis had their own problems with agreeing.

All humans in a physical body have only dealt with one of the lower Gods.

God does not deal with anyone from Hell until they can get out into the higher realms.

I know what people want to hear. They need to go out and pick up every other flowery book out there.

There are only a few religions that have a (spiritual exercise) that is needed to learn how to get out of the body. Wisdom and knowledge is needed to get into the higher realms. Both need to come from experience.

In all the paths that I have studied, I have never met anyone dealing with the real God. The deities will say whatever they must to win you over. Man is trying to say they are that here and now.

Most people want to make God human like. That means caring, loving and compassionate about all life. If one was willing to look at the truth, they would be seeing lies that have nothing to do with the truth of God. They like the world they create for themselves.

I will spend the rest of my days placing the truth against the lies of the greatest speakers. They promote themselves as if they were a little God speaking to God or that God spoke back. Many people try speaking to God.

Jesus could give any soul the sound and light to leave their body if they were ready and free of heavy karma. If they could have the experience they could be a true teacher and not just a follower.

It could be Lucifer's armies or alien soldiers that are stopping spiritual growth from happening.

People will not follow the Ten Commandments. They will follow their twisted Government laws or the ones they can make up. They all should be called Cults. Live by the laws you know are right.

A important topic that I feel should be mentioned. There is only a little about it in the Bible. I am speaking about the Ark of the Covenant.  There are people that say they have it or know where it is. If any Government knew where it was they would have it now. They would also have to keep it hidden for it would change the world in a way they would not want (without money and ego). There is nothing more powerful than that as far as Truth and power goes.

Man has nuclear bombs and lasers but they destroy indiscriminately. Nothing could destroy just the evil, as the Ark of the Covenant could.

I am sure people know if they have any evil inside them. I would bet to many people have very little truth from God, spirit or Jesus. They were never allowed to grow.

Surviving vs Salvation

What is man's desire really? All creatures of this world or realm care about survival. I know the word salvation sounds religious but I will give you a real definition.

When your life has real meaning, truth and a desire to understand God, anything else is the delusion or an illusion. Food, partying and sex will be the blocks you will face.

In a physical being the only thing that is important is eating. Next comes man's deep desire for sex, excitement and cheap thrills. Getting married was not important a long time ago. Being caring used to be a good trait. Being respectful was and is a very important part of life.

Salvation? what does that mean to people now? How do you get there? Why go through it? Are you being forced to? So many children are locked into programming about the Bible and Jesus. If your parents were not Christian is was Moses. The innovative New Age people are saying we are God or one with It.

All through history man uses torturing, killing and sacrificing to reach salvation. How is that? Any spiritual person was usually killed. Many times, by their own followers. Look at Jesus. Being torturing for how long? Look at Gandhi and other people being killed. The same as what the white man did to the Native people, as well as what happed to the Jewish people. Native people have no place to go home to because this is their home. The Quakers were also killed out.

No one has any right saying they are spiritual. Religion means controlling and killing. Which is what most religions have been doing since they were created by man. It says nothing in the Ten Commandments about creating a religion. It does say how to live within the ideas of earthly laws. Man assumes they are spiritual ones. Not man's created idea of what that should be.

The world needs guide lines to live by and if not, there is complete chaos and no control of any kind.

Since guns were created they are used for mostly killing. Even target practice is used to get better at what? Hitting something for what reason? To learn how to hit an animal or person to kill it? So, do you hear anything relating to God with that? No!

Killing and Torture

Let us look at the act of torture. Why do you think man always had to have an arena for people to fight in? It was always legal or excepted by everyone, except the people that were forced to play in it.

During the cowboy days, were there any morals? How about the saying "kill or be killed"? Did you ever wonder why that became part of life? Only a very few animals kill their opponent and don't eat them. It is for food only not pleasure.

Most people believe life is the important thing and will do anything to hold on to it. Killing is a big part of it.

Did God create sickness and disease? If It did why? Jesus taught about karma. Not that anyone was listening. Please don't ask anyone how real it is. You will get many ideas about it. Such as if you are bad you create it. Then I would ask you what is bad? Bad thinking or bad actions? What is a bad action? Not doing what most people feel is right or positive actions. That is always relative.

Killing is excepted for a person under man's idea of right. That alone goes against the Ten Commandments. If you don't believe in any of them, you must look at what is happening around the planet. If even one law was excepted, what would happen to the world? You are talking about only ten laws. How many laws are on the books right now?

Back to the idea of torture being excepted around the world. Do you have a clue to how animals inside the U.S. are killed, for food, for science and for entertainment? That alone shows man's spiritual growth is not happening.

LOVE

Most people believe love changes all things. If I may say not always for the better.

As an example, a relationship gone bad usually results in killing or extreme abuse. Love fades away in time for many. There's a desire for something better.

How does a person learn to understand love? I could go into all the things that I have learned the hard way.

I had three marriages and a total of eight girlfriends. I turned away from many before they started. I always had love or some level of it as a lifetime experience. It never happened the way I wanted it to. Many times, I wanted to die, and came close to.

Each person can usually control their emotions under normal conditions but not in a state of anger. Because that takes you out of any spiritual connection you have. Allowing very serious things to happen.

I am sure people around Jesus got angry for many distinct reasons. When a person takes it out on a person they say they love, really, how much did they really love that person? They say they loved God, Really?

Let's look at the Egyptians. They held immortalized. They had the ability the entire time to learn ascension. It was something they never did.

The greatest masters of the time had the Pyramids built for them. As if anyone ever came back to the physical with the same body they left in their last life. I am sure you can find many stories on that but that will be all they are.

Even Sri Baba's story came to an erupt end when he died from pneumonia in the hospital. Showing his truth was just that. He had one of the greatest following in the world while he was alive.

When it came close to Jesus being killed, (crucified) man's making it sound like it was an important way to go. It was the most barbaric way of human's revenge.

In The same way as the law kills killers for doing something they feel is wrong (murder) under their idea of right and wrong. Man's ideas are not close to any spiritual truth. I must say the most important law "thou shall not kill" means killing with no exceptions.

Man's mind is always on sex, even at the highest levels of all religions. Man's ideas say certain sex is dirty, but children are not born with that kind of programming. Man made sure it became a problem. (thanks to Moses).

How about facing the truth? The whole truth and nothing else? What is sex?

Do you believe what you see on TV, in the movies, or when you look outside your door? There are chemtrails over your head all the time and still they say it is not real.

What will it take? In the Devil's Advocate, Al Pacino says we are going to make the biggest mess until it reaches God and then IT will have to do something about it.

There are angels and deities to make sure none of that ever gets past the astral plane.

Are you going to see aliens or angels in your life time? Will you believe it? How do you prove to yourself it is real?

Are religion and spiritualism slowly being taken away? Is God becoming just an idea of how we want to be? Angels came here with a warning not to party. Are people with power good? Never.

These are the same people that agree with the U.S. sending an army into a country to blow up, destroy small towns and the families that live in them.

Man is the sickest evil creature walking this planet. Jesus tried to show them. They could leave this realm and go to a better place. He spoke about many different realms where killing is not present. It is the first step in becoming spiritual.

We are coming to the most incredible times in our history. The past is just that.

Christians are still waiting for Jesus to come back and save mankind. Really? He will come back, wave His hand, everyone will now follow and understand His truth? At the same time, how many Christians go to war and are killing people. It's totally against their own laws.

Man has the excuse that he can reincarnate again. Do people know how much about the earth changes every ten years never mind ever hundred years? Coming back to what? Trying to look deeper than the programmed ideas of what life is about, really, how many people are trying to understand?

When Jesus starting teaching about leaving the body most of his disciples could not understand. The idea of that meant dying to them. A very important truth was Jesus had only one way to prove to his followers what He was really teaching. As today I say if you did not have a true out-of-body-experience you will never truly understand much about the truth or soul, you cannot even prove it to yourself.

Many people are not able to have an out-of-body experience. It is the start of awareness of soul, and the beginning of a never-ending path.

What should be important to most people is what helps one understand God? I am sure most things one thinks and does, doesn't.

The action one takes, has everything to do with this world and keeping you here.

Lucifer would not want his children leaving him. Man thinks he knows God from what he reads and what other people tell him.

All the Preachers, Ministers, Rabbis, Priests, Shaman's and Medicine people speak an exceptional story. That is as far as it goes.

I stood before God. IT did not speak to me. Speaking would entail IT has a mouth and then except our words and truth. As if humans have any great understanding. I stood before God. If I said that what was given to me had anything to do with the earth I would be lying. I will tell you after that happened I could never be the same again.

When you have an experience never try to express to another. It will only take away from that experience.

I could not repeat what GOD said. If God wanted to speak to everyone IT would. They would have to understand God first. The first signs God gave us was treated as lies.

One of the most disrespected subject and words on the planet next to God is the

Ten Commandments. They are as real as it gets for God to speak to people. The translation was limited to man. There was more to each commandment. They were just the first part of the idea of each statement. There were twenty.  But it doesn't take a rocket scientist to know what is needed to be added to them.

Let's see what would Lucifer say to a person to try and win that person over? How does Lucifer even get you to that point of listening? What would It appear to you as? A giant creature, A giant animal, half animal and halve creature and half human? That are some of the images man worked with and created.

I use the word man more than humans for many reasons. In my truth, woman is much more connected in every way to spirit then men ever will be. In history, woman was not responsible for all the religions, fights and wars. Except for Joan Of Ark.

Dark entities and demons will come to anyone in the way they think they would want an angel to look like. They would not want to scare you, would they?

How about everyone is desperate and looking for a way out of what every they are stuck in, lost in, feeling lost and just desperate and depressed about. They are willing to do anything to get out.

The idea that Jesus will save them is important. Is it real or not being the real question?

That Lucifer will give one anything they want, real or not, is another false idea. It has its limit of what that is. If fame, fortune, money and sex are your wants, it can help you. It comes with so much karma you will stay here for many reincarnations.

When young people try to deal with things that they have no knowledge about, like death, angels and lucifer. They are fed lies. They are left so open for anything to happen. With no protection, lack of knowledge allows things to come into their reality and they just don't disappear. Who really teaches about real protection? If one truly knew Jesus it would be so different.

If you have the truth no one can interfere with your soul. If you have no real protection everything can and will. I am not speaking about your karma. We all live under world karma. When soul reaches any spiritual truth. It goes beyond the level of all life below it. This meaning demons, aliens and psychics. They all play with your awareness or lack of it.

I promote having the protection or the mind frame needed before you start.

I am sick of all the people speaking about meditation. They say clear your mind and go into nothingness. The other ones try to bring you somewhere. Where is that? A ship or place, saying we should meet the Galactic confederation, Why? What would be going on a ship do?

Going into oneness means what? Lose your self's identity? Lose your self-worth? Lose all the work you did in multiple lifetimes? You and everyone else are searching for what already is.

Can your teachers bring you to see God, something that you are not ready for? If you were you would not need a physical person to help you get there. What makes one think they deserve seeing God? Would anything that great, meaning God, really need your two cents?

People think they are important. One might be to their family but not to the world never mind God's worlds. Ego creates one's idea of power and self-worth.

The greatest inventors are given credit and fame for inventing something. It will not last long and then how important is it really? Are people looking at what they are really creating?

Tesla the greatest inventor has brought things to mankind that can and will destroy the planet. Again, he worked with an alien race.

People that have any kind of experience need to know from where it came. The mind, programs, drugs, bad dreams or even good dreams produce ideas and false experiences.

Jesus spoke about protection, He did protect many of His followers. The thing about that is it meant one's soul it is not the body.

John the Baptist gave everything to the truth about Jesus. He did know where he was going to go when they chopped off his head. He was already prepared.

One must decide what they want to create or the reality they will try to live in. One must relate to man-made ideas. In that the rich people created the laws most of us must live by. Rich people don't care about middle class or poor people. What about the rich that have their own islands and communities? They can live in La-la land. Living in the dream. Telling themselves it is real.

Again, I must say what Jesus said more than three times, "I know it is easier for a camel to go throw an eye of a needle then a rich person to get into heaven".

The scientists of today have no way to understand God so they must attack IT. I am not like most people. Science will never help man understand God. It will never help us understand anything more about love. It might help a little about earth if they could listen to their own truths. They still are going ahead with Chemtrails and the Haarp system. Let's not forget all the weapons they keep making and are trying to use.

Do they think they will be able to beat alien races in any battle? Yes, they do. They also know some races can just wipe us out if they decide to.

What does man really care about? Should they go out and use Viagra? They can have sex for hours. In their programmed minds, yes. Do you think it is a mistake having an erection for more than four hours? The truth will stop it all.

Scientists have been programmed with an idea of what people think they want God to be. The same as they cannot speak about the truth behind many things like the space program.

The newer part of all this has become alien abduction. Christians like to use the word demons for aliens. Many new agers call Jesus an alien, not that we are all not that, but that doesn't make Jesus any different than any other Human. He was the only one to prove how soul moves on. He did not try to make people stay here like everyone else is doing. Even that is a two-sided sword. They are creating more sickness for everyone every day.

Man ate very little many years ago. The links (between, man and ape) or between man and monkey still have no real connection to each other. They never did and never will. People follow those ideas, including the earth is flat and we never went to the moon.

Change never made man different. They never became something different and science cannot understand that. The search for the missing link was never really found because it does not exist.

There were many different races here after Atlantis. There were many before as well. They were also brought here not born here. Humans did not pop out of a meteorite or get created by it. Because we have the same elements doesn't make us the same.

Carbon also has nothing to do with Soul. Lucifer is not carbon based. Nor are the deities of the inner worlds.

Alien knowledge has taken the secret Government beyond Einstein's thinking. His knowledge was not proven to be close on many levels.

Tesla already gave us the most advanced knowledge to hit this planet. His work took us many years into the future. Nothing is as good as it sounds. All his inventions are making the earth unsafe really. Many people will differ on that. If they knew what he really brought to man. He brought the first radio as well as an earth quake machine and a doomsday weapon.

I feel it seems like it will be about one or two more years before the world will know about aliens. I feel this beyond a shadow of doubt. I am not saying it will be anything good.

No two people will ever understand the same thing in the same way. Never mind except it. I say, repeatedly you need your own experience.

I am speaking about death experiences, out-of-body, psychic experiences and even meeting with things not of this world. That is beings that are not solid (transparent). It is not about anything except your truth. You need to create your truth by experience. Not reading or listening to someone else's.

Jesus was never a solid physical body when He came back to His followers after being crucified. The people that say they met Him did not understand that right away. If Jesus came back now He could not help the planet. I see a major disaster coming that will. I am talking about the balance the earth needs.

I am a realist. I am soul. I am an incarnitiate. That means being aware of all my past lives and understanding them.

In the beginning of religions, the Hindu's believed that Shiva came during the flood to re-create Humans. He is called the destroyer and creator. The highest

God. Shiva says He is the greatest God to humans. He is one God that many other people give different names. It is accepted as being part of a religion or I would call a program.

Life is all the mind games about what man thinks it can do and create. Humans cannot create soul, only the body it uses to move around in the physical can. That will become very important in the future. Because one's attention will be focused on just that.

Now for the hard truth. Why did God put you in Hell? Lucifer is the main controlling factor now in power over it. WHY? Think about that one.

When one starts learning about self they need to learn everything about soul. The first and most important is what you are as soul and what you are not. Good or bad is real and man will not even except that.

If you live to be very old. How old will you be and why will you die? Right now, it is one-hundred- twenty- five years. There is no proof.

Ego is starting to be part of everything and not in an effective way. It makes you believe all the lies and stories you are being told, shown and taught. Instead of helping, you create more. I don't blame Lucifer for giving people their own truth back to them. Everything must be worked out some way. You must pay back for what you think your gifts are when it comes to the physical. Any gift you have here is nothing to what you are going to have when you get into the higher levels /rooms in the inner worlds.

We all have demons and aliens creating a world that has nothing to do with being spiritual. To work at becoming spiritual, one most learn a few spiritual laws and you really don't need that many. Here are five. You do have to adapt them into your life. We will start with the most important law. If you don't you will never see the higher realms.

#1 - The Law of Non-interference. Meaning not inviting yourself into anyone's situation without being asked in by them. You can be invited in many ways and at many various levels, physical, astral or even in the higher realms. There must be a true connection on the other side of the action, by their higher self.

a.     soul's awareness is different in each of the different bodies it will use, depending on the realm it is in.

b.     It will take on an astral body with the mental body being as real as your physical body is here is to you now.

c.     You have a body on each plane or Realm. At this very moment working at the same time. Your awareness comes from the lowest body you are in ninety-nine percent of the time. That is unless you are out of the body. That is the most important thing you can learn in this life time.

#2 - The Law of Truth. Soul's obedience to God. All systems need a higher power. All systems do have a higher power except for that of God Itself. No system can run for long without it.

  a. That is also for all angels, deities and beings, not just people.

#3 - The Law of Soul and the bodies it uses. It is based on karma in the astral world. Then it changes to awareness in the next realm.

Awareness is just responsibility. Its proving your self-worth.  I don't hear many people speaking about that either. Unless it is working to get a so called better job.

  a. Things soul can do and the things it is not yet allowed to do. Killing being only God's right on any level. The deities that are given God power over a realm is different than peoples.

b. Their abilities change for each soul when one's awareness changes. I am sure many people think that is unfair.

People have been programmed to think that we are all equal. Science is still trying to prove that.

Someone without sight cannot be compared to one with it, physical or psychically. I am not saying they cannot have incredible experience different than most for they do.

We have so many unaware people. You may call lost souls. They are creating so much karma for themselves and the world. Do you have the right to stop them? You can and need to create protection for you and yours.

#4. -The Laws of each realm. Each world or realm is so different. Each body you move into in that realm is different.

Only realization of one's own awareness in it will help each soul learn the laws of each realm. It's then you can use them.

Everything you think you are learning here has nothing to do with the next realm. Are your ears closed to that? Think about it?

#4 You may look at a law as a restriction. Such as it is here. There you are free. Each law there allows you things you can do here. The things you never had or could not do before.

#5 -The Law of the Universe is abused by all living beings. The laws of atoms and learning to work with it not against it. If science was using the mind of a gifted child they would use them in a destructive way.

These Laws are not accepted by most people, most people feel they are above them. In that case, they will always stay below them.

Man, with his ego will say we don't need someone else's laws, God's or not!

The karma one creates can only be paid back by oneself. A few actions that cannot be paid off in lifetimes such as killing and abuse. Only a few souls I know in history have ever reached that. Jesus did not have other karma other than earth's karma.

It is many lifetimes since Jesus's teachings and only few people now understand it. The way the world has changed shows they don't want his truth. It is not what people thinks it should be. It is not just love, compassion and peace.

Now days with people excepting any vision or experience with an alien or demon. They except whatever they hear.

I will tell my short story. I was gifted, many say they are. I would say comparing people that did not experience God to one that did is crazy. It's important being able to speak about truth with full knowingness. That is gifted. I am not speaking about being a healer by any means. I am speaking about knowing one's truth, that being what they are to God.

When I was in Atlantis it was my first incarnation on this planet. It was the Garden of Edan. In the end, it was destroyed. I could not understand that. I had to come back. It was like trying to see humans starting over having everything then losing it.

I had to learn all the new religions and all the new lies. Lifetime after lifetime. I did get stuck in all the religious ideas of ego and beliefs. I had to know them all. Until my lifetime when I was with Jesus when He had a physical body.

After seeing the birth of Sarah and seeing what happened to Jesus' followers, I knew it was time to say good bye to them as well. I was in the same space I was in when I knew Atlantis was going to be destroyed.

How can people perpetuate something so evil to their own race and to their own world? I did not understand why the people next to Jesus help kill Him.

Only the loves in my life and the present relationship, that went beyond sex, is what allowed me to see what happened in Atlantis and to Jesus.

Each soul needs to find out their answers. You will know everything about your karma when you find your answers to life.

There is a catch twenty-two. If you are working from a spiritual level you cannot abuse any laws of God that you know. If you abuse the laws here you really are abusing the higher laws as well.

Life here is dependent upon a person being aware of the laws and trying to become spiritual. This by no means involves dis-owning spiritual laws.

Being a good person doesn't mean you are a spiritual person. Most good people don't follow the spiritual laws or even the Ten Commandments. It doesn't matter what religion they say they are in. That is scary.

Abuse is the most dangerous thing for creating karma and next is killing.  I should say, anything done against the name of GOD is the main way to create karma. It is the third commandment. The Commandment is not bad and doesn't create war or fighting.

I am not sure why people are listening to the words of the Bible as truth. I found so many major discrepancies in all their writings.

People that think the Ten commandments are spiritual laws they are not. They are earth laws to live by. If you live by them you will not create karma here on earth. How many people even know them or want to follow them? I said I would give them to you.

Ten laws of earth.  2x

One, Only one God. Follow no other gods. Most of history is based on alien gods. Man was given to many false Gods to follow, like a child in a candy store.

Two, No, images of God or likes. Not that anyone can even try to make one. How many people truly understand anything about the way God looks? Through all my studies no religion does. Man accepts Man's idea of Jesus being God so all they can relate to is another man-made idea of who and what God is. Making It a compassionate, loving being. That is not even close. If It were the world would be different.

Three, You, cannot speak bad against God or curse God (you can!). Funny, most people do that every day. How many don't even say they are sorry when they do. They don't even face it.

Four, A holy day. Are you serious? Why? Spirit knew man could not occupy his mind any longer than a day or even a few hours. People try going into a retreat for years. Does one really think they need to speak to anything that long and still not be able to understand It, really? Telling remarkable stories doesn't mean anything without proof. On Holy days even giving one hour to God was difficult. If they did pray it was always an action of begging God for something.

The Dali Lama preaches peace. He left his country because he would have been killed. He travels the world speaking about peace. People say if he did not, his message would have never gotten around the world.

These teachings originated in ancient India. Teachings that are not much different than all the New Age religions speaking about peace. Dreaming is for dreamers. Life is only for living in action.

I was always protected from killing or being killed. There were times I wanted to kill. In another life time, in Tibet, there was a serious war going on and I was too little to fight. I still got killed when the small town I was in was attacked. My father in that life lived hundreds of years longer. I did see him in my present life before he died in this life time.

What is a teaching if it cannot teach anything that they can be proven? They teach how to pray then to who? If one does pray are they helping the planet? Does it help anyone or anything? Determining which souls need what teachings are given to the lower deities that teach a few souls at a time. They do not work with just anyone. Everything you get spiritually, you must earn. That is not just by praying.

The saying which is more important your wife or your child? Compare that to the people of the U.S. to the people of Africa? Saving the earth or a part of it? Do you think one soul is more important than any other soul? Man looks at certain souls as important over many others. Should love over ride spiritual laws? Never.

Any soul with awareness is worth saving. They will save many more souls then most of the people of earth put together will.

Many souls don't realize they are unaware of their potential. What they need is a little spark to be awakened.

Jesus came for the few not the many. He came for the soul's ready to grow not stay stagnant. He said, "He who have little faith follow Me". Why? They were already looking but just not aware. When one becomes aware you can start reading people's aura and start seeing and hearing the truth if there is any.

In the scenario of a sinking ship. The woman and children leave first. Then the men and lastly the Captain of the ship. The captain of the ship should go down with it.

The double-sided sword is that any master should be able to give their life for their student. The same as any student of a true master should be able to give their life for their teacher. If not, ego is the problem of the one that won't.

The desire for world peace, Why? You are not in heaven or anything even close to it. You are totally on the opposite side of it.

Five, honor your mother and father, only if, the honor is returned. Meaning parents expect their children to give them respect. One must earn respect before it is returned. You would not give a child a gun until they could use it properly. Respect is important to give as it is to receive. If they don't learn respect people get hurt or killed. Do people respect anything anymore really?

Six, no killing, there is no cause or excuse to killing. Anger is the one thing that allows it to happen. It is the one thing that takes you out of the connection with spirit. Anything can happen and usual does from bad to violent. Wars and family fights take out many good and bad people, out of ignorance and lack of awareness of God. Seven, no adultery. Do people respect life or understand the consequences if they go against it? It has nothing to do with young or old. Just the amount of karma one creates. One will never be forgiven in this lifetime. That is in the Bible if anyone really wants to read it. Jesus did say what actions create the most karma.

Man's ego allows oneself to create their own laws and beliefs, wrong as they usually are. If one thinks aliens or entities can help is another mistake. You are alone when you step onto the spiritual path. Lucifer will offer one many things and they will usually take them.

Eight, no right to steal. That is for anyone in anyplace. Being forced into it has something to do with one's karma. Karma that has already been created. They think they have found a better way to pay it off. It is never right. Was the idea of Robbin Hood good or bad? It depends on earth laws or spiritual laws.

Nine, no false witness against another. So many people trying to pass blame on someone else. Most men are afraid to face their own faults and deeds. They are always trying to give it to someone else. It does not work that way and will never. Hells laws are just for this world or realm

Ten, you cannot covet someone else - no one or any of their things. We are each responsible for what we have and how we use that. Not how we use other people's things including one's husband or wife. It is a fundamental problem.

Let's see, which one of these laws is bad for human's way of living? I don't see any. Never mind Love is not mentioned, there is it? Jesus was not born on the earth yet. Through His life, love took a giant step because of the way Jesus showed love for His wife Mary Madeline. I met a few people aware of their lives with Jesus as well. They all agree with me. Do you really need to wonder why?

Many people don't understand the spiritual worlds as separate from the physical world. Man's programed ideas about it all being one. I would always reply it is a down right lie.

Everything man makes or creates, he thinks it is something greater, name one thing? The house we live is no better made then what they use to live in. Most races or tribes stopped living in strong houses, moving into wood, skin and even plastic instead of stone. Things of the past could survive thousands of years now. Things start breaking down after a hundred years.

Jesus never spoke about building in the physical even though his father was a master carpenter. He never said churches had to be built. He used metaphors for that. Man could not even translate that into the truth. Jesus sent His disciples around the world and I am sure many were mistaken for Jesus. How easy to just change your name if you needed to hide.

Talking about out of body experience, you can say you went anywhere you want and even believe it. Did you even look at your own body? What body were you in? Did you look like you did in this world and the same age? Were you different in any way?

Soul uses five bodies in the lower worlds. Your awareness level decides what body you will step into when you leave here. Age is usually set within a certain range. Yes, you can stay locked in a program always.

Are you aware enough to use your truth? Jesus sent many of His followers around the world. They left with nothing other than their truth. Why are people today afraid to even say what theirs is?

So many people thinking they are here helping the world become what? My MAIN PURPOSE IS HELPING SOULS THAT WANT TO LEARN HOW TO PREPAIR AND TAKE THEIR NEXT STEP, INTO THE NEXT WORLD!

I call this world hell while I am here. Who was the first teacher to teach truth. It is not as old as people think. All the truth from the beginning was nothing close to being important. It is not now so how could it be then?

In my first book, How to See God. I mention about Jesus being with Mary but did not want to go into detail. The Da Vinci code came out a week later. Which brings out the idea Jesus might have had a child. Even that was covered up.

All souls learn by their own experiences important or not. That is not everyone for many never get their first important experience. Many of you did at least once in another life and some people did many times before in one of their lifetimes. It is a shame you don't remember any of it. Lucifer, learned his real place in the lower worlds. He is not going against God. He went through that fire already. He is happy being where he is like many people are happy being here. He can do what he is does because God allows him to and not for any other reason.

The Pope recently said he wants more people to start doing exorcisms. He hired over 1,500 people to do them. I have a good friend who is doing about three-hundred a year. I did some in my lifetime. The most ridiculous thing the Pope said was Hell doesn't exist. He doesn't even know he is living in it.

Very few people can be a real exorcist. Why? They have no truth. They lack any real connection to Jesus and God. Just saying it doesn't make it real. As so many clams their dreams are. The first movie the exorcist was based on a real story, except it was a boy not a girl. People died during it.

Look at two new TV series. One is called the Exorcist and the other Lucifer. There is so much information being given out. It's very interesting ideas about things outside the box or programed ideas most people have. So many false ideas are excepted as truth out there.

Many don't think they should follow the older ideas as well. Many believe they are better than that. Demons are not real. What a sick perverted idea coming out of one's ego. Religions have bastardized all the laws they are supposed to live by. As well as the programming that most men get from all the wrong things. Thinking man came first over woman. I feel is one of the main reasons that has destroyed man from moving forward and trying to create a world of harmony.

Dr Lyall Watson 1938-2008 came out with this story. It was only partly true. It was the hundredth monkey theory. People want to believe it. I will tell you. The opposite is happening with one million people would that not change too if it were true? It would be in a cycle where one would never catch up to the other.

Jesus tried to give His followers the next step in spiritual growth and unfoldment. Love is just one small part of it. He could only show that through His actions. That is the only way one can truly understand a love. Words do not explain love by any definition. All the feelings we deal with can come from good or unpleasant experience, like crying, yelling, sex or laughing. The reaction is different for different people based on their experience. Not one person can say what love really is in the physical world that would agree with everyone else a hundred percent.

When we go out into the world, like Jesus said we go out as sheep among the wolves. Do people have a clue to what that means? It does not mean go out and get a machine gun and then gun all your enemies down or you will die. It doesn't mean become a super hero which only means one's ego is bigger than the body it is in. It allows them to go against all the true spiritual laws.

When standing on earth it is hard to call it anything other than life. People call it heaven.

People can call the ocean, the trees, the mountains, the lakes and the animals beautiful.

I would have to say woman are first. Woman move on into the higher worlds and the others do not.

In the animal kingdom, the males are prettier. With birds, the males are prettier. They have more colorful feathers. With fish, it is the same. They have more colors on their fins and tails. Women desire to try to be prettier always.

Most of Jesus' teachings fell on barren soil. Saying you follow Jesus, or God to do what? People speaking about God like (He) is watching them and helping them. To do what? Save the world from what? It sure is not sexual abuse, rape, murder, starvation, even perverted or twisted love. That doesn't even take in what they do to the earth, It's forests, rivers, streams, oceans, lakes, animals, creatures, birds, fish and its mammals. It sure has nothing to do with what man is doing to children, physically or psychically. Man controls the voting system, woman do not, I don't agree with that and that is a problem.

How can man think fighting and killing is still accepted?

Where is the purity of the heart? The spiritual heart. I am not speaking about the physical heart. They are not the same.

Soul doesn't have any physical organs it does not need them.

If you are looking for a real religious teaching here on planet earth here it is.

Sin is the same as Karma. Man will come to a time when he decides to try and create Good Karma. Man tries to make everything sound good. All a person's karma must be paid off not just taken away from them or it will be traveling with you even after your body dies.

If you keep taking money out on a credit card. Sooner or later it will come to a point where it will have to be paid or you will lose it. (along with the things that come from it will). The only good feeling is paying it off.

People killing is crazy now. Man thinks he can kill the bad people and it is a good thing.

I say look at two boxers going into the ring. They both pray to beat the other person up. Who do you think they are praying to? One usually wins so is Jesus or God favoring that person? I am sure the ones fighting think so. Do they understand karma? They must think they are skipping karma.

Man thinks anything is ok, if they get other men to agree. Do you think you can hurt anything or anyone intentionally and not create karma? Making money on it doesn't make it right but it does create karma.

I had to learn many things the hard way over and over. The truth is like Jesus' story about turning your cheek. You have heard it repeatedly. Two wrongs don't make a right. Man, still has not learned that lesson. You need to ask yourself why?

Man is holding on to the body, the earth and whatever else one thinks they have. Lucifer wants to keep people here. In his mind imagine how many people he thinks he has control over? I would estimate seventy-five percent at least of the planet.

Look at Russia, China and Germany armies being created. There are also the smaller countries playing with bombs. That is destroying any idea of creating peace. That sure doesn't increase love either.

When it comes to God, why is it all religions force their ignorant ideas of God on all their followers? Saying how many children you should have. They are allowing killing for the right reason. How many times one can get married. How much money you are supposed to give and to who God or the church? Their God demands money. Lastly, what you are supposed to believe. You should only believe what you know as truth nothing else should really matter. Then ask yourself the question. Are any of those things right or even important for spiritual growth?

We are all here on this planet now. If we cannot live together here we will not be able to anywhere else either. Your dying, will not make it right and if you are coming back you will see nothing changed. You will not even know what happened.

What I will suggest is getting involved with anything to help this world in anyway. I do not support the things that cause the problems of the world.

All this has nothing to do with the severe problem of aliens programming earth people either. That will not be revealed to the world soon enough to help change it.

Week minded people that are open to ideas are very easy to fill with false ones. It is about helping the insanity to get better not making it worse. They are leading many people down a dark road. All the so called, spiritualists, and religionists more than ever are the ones creating the biggest problems.

Jesus said in the end times there will be more false Prophets than ever in history. All I see and hear every day is we are at that point right now.

If you think I am crazy, I am but I am going sane. How many people will swear on their life's truth? My family is gone. There is no one to swear on. I do to God and that is the highest one can go.
How many can say they stood with Jesus? Then say they Stood before the real GOD. They are not the same. (Not the man-made idea of a loving God) either.

The world is following the ghosts of the past. Moses brought the world down a level instead of bringing them up. He was supposed to raise people up and out of the lower level everyone was in. Whether you believe much about the Bible and all the other man-made stories. We are still sinking fast. All the written tablets, do you understand a person wrote them?

If you don't, do you except the idea about One race of the giants that are called the (Annunaki) and accept it as a real story? Do you accept how they re-created man? I beg you to think about that. Things will happen soon and they will pull more people into the lies.

Time is changeable now. Imagine changing things whenever you did not like certain events that happened. How many different ideas would people come up with now? It would still not help mankind at any level. Ego of the world is in power and that is controlled.

What about humans has changed in two-hundred-thousand years, except the stories they believe? The stories they tell and the entities that they follow change. Does that help?

Who really can tell you about the first idea of any kind of God? Then in the beginning how long was it before man starting writing? Why were the first symbols pictures of animals, dinosaurs, half animal and creature beings? Have you ever wondered why?

Why is it, in all the important stories, there was an authentic experience attributed to the person who brought out that message. Then the event happened. The few stories like Noah and the Ark and Sodom and Gomora are examples.

The four gospels were twisted by two evangelists. Luke and Mark, who worked with Peter and Paul. Only Matthew and John of the New Testament were Jesus' true disciples. Most people have no clue to that and how twisted it was. They will twist that and come up with they are God. If not that, they are saying they are one with It. Really? Show me one person that can fit that and have any kind of proof. They were there trying to control the story that will be fed to the people.

Lucifer's army always had control over the physical worlds for a very long time. Not sure how many aliens even know that and why they are doing it. Who knows what to do about that, anyone?

I never heard anyone speak about God from the knowledge given to them from aliens that had any real importance. The only repeated lie is they are here to help us when we are ready. Does everyone lack any real thinking?

Can you see what a sick world this is now? I know everyone is looking for the silver lining. So many sick people and sick laws to live by. Everything is contaminated. Our life supporting environment is dying.

U.S. court systems that control many things we do, seems to be allowing rapist to get off easier than they should and many are serving only months instead of years. I feel they need life sentences. Anyone that is involved with rape should read the Bible.     Jesus's teachings spoke about things that cannot be forgiven. The karma that murder gives a person.

Mother Teresa went against that by spending her last few years trying to rehabilitate killers. Right before she died she started doubting God herself. She was hanging with killers for two years. She was thinking she was doing God's work which had a very serious toll on her. Doubting God after all the years of her life dedicated to IT.

Even the courts do not use a Bible or anything to do with God. I wonder why?

Now we have Trump and we will face the biggest disaster the world has ever seen. In his own words. Putin is one of the richest person on the planet, meaning he can do anything he wants and who will stop him? Yesterday they used the God word in court. It was on TV.

What about nuclear wars? They are becoming very dangerous to the people of the world.

Man, is getting away with too many things on those issues of abuse. It is not even a crime any more. They get little jail time if they get any. There are so many cases with people watching and nothing happening to the perpetrator. I cannot see anything other than Lucifer taking over man's own ego. I see it as growing bigger and making people go insane. The sickness is not getting smaller.

I am not sure people understand the Muslim religion, they better read up on the Quran and learn about it. Just a few months ago they passed a law where the Husband can beat his wife. It just gets sicker as you learn more. Which Mohammad created with Gabriel? Was it really Gabriel? Who is that?

They believe they don't go to heaven if they get killed by a woman. I think we need a woman army to fight there. Imagine how many will no longer want to die by a woman's hand.
Where are these people's God? In Gabriel hands?

I am asking you to do this again, to see if after reading what I have shared with you thus far, if any of your ideas changed?

I will ask you to write down on a piece of paper what God is and what IT isn't? List everything It is on one side and everything IT isn't on the other.  Also write what feelings you think God has.

Now do the same thing with whatever you know or even think you know about Jesus. That means you cannot just say He is everything.  How can you believe anything if you don't know what you don't know? Or even think you know what you don't know

Who do you follow in truth? Are they angels or demons in an earth body costume? How about flying as a super powered ego?

An idea people will try so hard not to face is the dark side, but love the good side of all things. Whatever people perceive that to be is man's programmed image.

Many people think we all get into heaven, after three million years there are many more souls here then the next realm and many less in the realm after that. Most seem to want to stay here all the time.

You're in a programmed world and nothing is important except your programmed idea of truth. It is this easy, look at the real world listen to the news on the computer or TV and see what is really going on.

How important is truth? Depends on who's. Yours, Lucifer's or God's.

The Tesla car can almost self- drive itself, is that better? How many children are waiting to be able to drive? That was the way it was for normal children in the past. We can now sit back and tell the car to drive. While you sit back, do what drugs and drink?

Most inventions destroy the planet in some way. Man keeps taking energy from inside the earth. They say that there are tons more to take. Prove it. Is it ok? They tell us the ocean is ok, really?

The movie exorcist (new one) this week showed how people don't understand the truth and will do anything to hide from it.

Take your truth to the highest level, whatever level you think that is. Then compare that to what everyone is saying. Is it the same or is it different?

Everyone must learn their own truth. That is half right and half wrong. Your own truth just means the level that you are willing to except. The truth itself doesn't ever change. Just your ability to understand it.

Consciousness is not SOUL. So many teachers, teach you that. People speak about tapping into the one conciseness. If that were the case that would mean consciousness is a very sick entity within Itself.

Why would any of the so-called spiritual teachers here be clones? Many say go within yourself. Many say they do, but no one comes out with anything important. After many life times, after I was with Jesus. I was only able to put my truth together in the past ten years. I'm am now only understanding the reason for everything. Why I kept reincarnating changed into incarnating for the last time.

The difference is being aware of the knowledge you had before you came here. It's being able to move forward from that point. When that happens, one doesn't go backwards. If one does, everything you do creates twice as much Karma.

Soul's thoughts are not like the minds are. Soul knows everything it needs to and must always fight the mind to get it through into the consciousness. Every experience one has is attacked by the mind. Mind usually wins, then the experience is dismissed as normalcy. That is why man has very little understanding of soul's past lives.

The next problem is man usually makes the wrong decision in an emergency. Most listen to the consciousness of a programmed brain. I never said they were the same. They are not.

You always have two trains of thought. One is mind and the other is soul. One is always right and the other is partially right sometimes. You always have two different outcomes. Wow, what if one could always know the best decision? I am sure they would make it unless influenced by drugs, drinking or anger.

Was Moses already working for Lucifer? When you are speaking about Moses it seems God is blamed for what happened to the people.

Whoever created that false truth in the first place? They are the ones to be blamed. That means the people saying they are religious and the ones in power which were programmed. They could never tell the truth If God Itself gave it to them. They would call it their higher self. I call it Ego. It has become man's new God. It is now called consciousness or oneness.

Oneness

Why would anyone want to be one with any creature, plant or animal? To run faster, to eat better, to grow bigger, to think they have any spiritual knowledge is even more crazy. They are all bound to the physical laws. They are in a direct relationship with the rain, the snow, the wind, the temperature, and all the other creatures. They cannot pray or even leave their bodies. Some animals can dream. All their actions are natural. The amount of love they experience is limited to those laws and how much man interferes.

Being one with all people, why? The first problem is thinking we are all the same. Science keeps saying that. Spiritualist say that as well. Well are you a tiger, a bear or an ant? People are so different. They keep trying to be the same. Being black, red, yellow or white is different. When they have children with each other only the strongest genes survive which decides features of what race will be dominant. In another few years all that will change. Then you can say we are all one (race).

Soul has its own level of awareness that is so different than the mind. To assume we are equal is so sickening to hear. Yes, we all eat and breath. Some people are more than that.

If you are one with dreadful things, why? Why would you want to be equal to a rich person? So that you could have everything you think you want. If you just repeat their action, you will become that. Then you are one with them. If you refrain from those actions you are not one with them. You are becoming aware.

This you need to learn over everything else, what the importance of moving forward from the physical level to the higher levels are. In the higher worlds of God, there are five, with each having three realms in each. They each have a different importance to soul. They are each what soul needs to learn and then move beyond that realm.

Why not learn about God and then start trying to be one with that? No, it has nothing to do with just loving people. I mentioned what Mother Terisa went through already. Why not give up what you learned from someone else's stupid ideas. In any decision, there are always two ways to go and one is better than the other. My truth is not stupid if you understand it.

In this world of over seventy-two billion people do you think they all want to except the same thinking or be like everyone else?

Jesus taught much more about death than He did about life. Man thinks the opposite.

The Egyptians were aware about death being important but they had no one to teach them about it after the aliens left. With all their God's and teachers, they truly did not understand reincarnation or death.

All the new age thinkers are more concerned about the Universal energy than Gods. I think that will slowly destroy humanity no matter what life forms they say they are working with. They will just become slaves all over again.

Soul must agree with letting go of the physical body completely meaning forever. If you hold on to that idea or that consciousness you will keep reincarnating here. Where you place your awareness, soul will usually go there right or wrong. You can stay here even when you become aware. If you do you then must think you are better than God.

Jesus taught the steps to each higher world and that awareness. He never tried to make this world right. Free will is the illusion of this world. The idea of heaven being here, even Moses was ignorant thinking that. It will never be or will the astral plane be, because of man's own destructive nature and twisted ego.

Aliens are so much older than humans. All races here came from other worlds. Just look at what they did here. What good did man ever do for earth? I guess most people would say build pyramids. They have never learnt about God's worlds or God Itself. They would rather play with the lower aliens, deities and demons. If one was truly working with higher forms they would not want to stay here to make this world better.

Something very important is sex. It is the deadliest act in this realm. It can bring you to an elevated level of love. It can also bring you into the darkest parts of this realm and into the most perverted ideas and actions. It only exists in the lower realms. The lower deities play in it. Aliens play in it as well as the Giants and every creature here does. Many of the acts are perverted. Some animals need sex as much as men do. They act so much like humans and don't even care if it is a human. The same as man is becoming more animalistic every day. You can see that by what people watch.

The Giants had sex with the little people. The Deities had sex with people. Aliens love sex with humans. They would be happier to have us for dinner.

Are you following me? Can you think of something important man has done in one-hundred years, meaning spiritual? Did any angel or alien make that any different?

Mankind keeps saying he is building a better world, a faster car and a stronger house is better. Are they even better than the pyramids, really? Using advanced tools, to do what build or destroy?

The substances we use like oil and plastic are becoming the main substances for everything that used to be wood and even steel. It is destroying our oceans and our health.

Jesus taught about giving everything up not how to get more of it. He always said the rewards are in Heaven not here.

When you are in first grade what do you really know about anything? Then over the next ten years you are being programmed with what? How important something is based on someone's idea?

Jesus came in as a wrecking ball, like Miley Cyrus sings. He came in as the burning bush. The wrath of God's fire and Brimstone. He came to tear down the lies not build them up. Man was not ready.

Very few people want to understand God, they want God to understand them. Still not realizing at that point they are dealing with a lesser God called ego.

One thing, church people are a little more caring about each other no matter what is being said, at least for a few hours a week.

When it comes to war. Man, has a problem and again it is called ego. Jesus spoke about the chosen people as the people that believe in God. It is the truth for me. Not the wanna-bes that the Native people, call the white people trying to be Native. I have not been called that.

I was respected on every reservation I was on. I lived in South Dakota for a short while. No one tribe has more of God's truth than any other path. All filling in what they don't know with aliens and scientist's ideas.

People that think planet earth is heaven or even important. They will have a genuine problem with trying to save it. It doesn't need to be saved. God created a heaven here but sadly man destroyed it. Hell is here for a reason now. I am sure man doesn't want to know what that reason is.

Man, was programmed to kill over twenty-thousand years ago. That has not changed in any aspect. Look at people. They cannot even keep a relationship. To think all that is happening without alien's influence. Many UFO people will say the opposite.

Moses' God was real and is still here. It is one of the three Gods in the third world. It has most everything under Its control. Including most of the alien races.

Lucifer is there on top of the astral world as well. The fallen angels of God are all there too. Do any aliens really care about our problems? They do care about their problems. What is their ultimate goal?

The war is imminent. I don't really want to see people killing children when there is no reason to. Earth has sunk so much deeper into the darkness over the past one-hundred years and now people think they are more spiritual now than ever before. To stop killing, you must learn about killing, like the angels that learned that is not the answer and because of that, they were thrown out of the third realm into the Astral plane. Man is not better by any means no matter what they think or tell themselves.

You don't have to experience killing someone to know it is wrong. You may think you do. You already experienced many things in many other lifetimes and still you want to do them again.

Satin is coming in full force now. It is not of Jehovah teachings. Even that was only a little better.

What do you want in life (everything?) then sell your soul to the devil. You won't have to worry about it until it is time to pay it all back. When you decide to leave the lower world. If you like living here it is no problem then.

Jesus did free many people from the bond of earth. More people could have been if they listened. They were all ready to let go of everything. They were not holding on to things like most people still are.

I have a challenging time when people do not speak about death in a realistic way. Nothing about death, which is something everyone will go through no matter what they do think or say.

They have a max of one-hundred and twenty-five years at most. Unless they do create a way of storing your consciousness in a machine. At that point, will you be able to stop them from doing that to you? It would be like Einstein's brain in a bottle. Imagine people being able to use your awareness to do something after your body is gone. Well hopefully that will be stopped before it becomes a complete reality. You are out of control in a body never mind being out of it.

A so called spiritual person says be present in the moment, what one, the dream land one or the real one? How about being aware of what is really happening. Now more children dying from so many man-made things. What would Jesus say?

I just listened to a famous speaker who is a millionaire speaking about living in the moment. He had no understanding of death. A so-called spiritual person asked Him about death. How can one be preaching not knowing about death? It proves he knows nothing about life. They both go together.

His remark was his mother and father died. Speakers never speak about a real world. How can you speak about life without any knowledge of death and truth?

With all the speakers, so called spiritual people speak about everything that doesn't help the world. They create false hopes in people about death. Every Prophet, Spiritualist, Sharman, Medicine person all live in a dream or try to bring people into their Fantasy world.

People saying, they are channeling angels like:

Metatron - channeling Him really?

People using all the names of the angels in the Bible and then even making a few more up.

People might not realize demons never use their real names. It would be easy to find out that they are not the angels they say they are. Listen to any message one gets.

I am sure these speakers don't know who they are really working with. They are speaking to such a small part of the population, so programmed they believe their own story. They truly think they are making a difference. It is easy to live in dreamland and tell everyone that dream. If you say your dream is real and it is wrong one day you will find your karma waiting for you.

All people through history creating a dream world and it is no closer to being real now than it was two-hundred years ago.

Jesus gave us truth. Something no one else could. A true understanding of death. Why man dies. His whole death was to show that and He proved it to us. Man, will always be trying to pay off their karma. It cannot be but for trying you might get more karma.

A wealthy writer can pay to have the number one book. I would never spend money to create a lie. Guess what? They get super publicity and the book becomes a best seller overnight.

With over seven billion people here today and most are starving and homeless how many people do these speakers really think they are speaking to? How will that change the world at any level? They would have to learn what spiritual means not man's created idea of it.

Why do so many channelers and psychics insist on using one of the angel's name out of the Bible? I am sure most people don't know much about angels really. Even less of what Jesus was really teaching which could help them understand angels.

In the Muslim religion, they speak about Mohammad talking with Gabriel. Was he a good angel? How much did that angel know about a real God when He was cast out of the higher realm just like Lucifer?

Look at the world and the way people were living then compared to how they are living now. Before the world changes for the better, a lot must change, like everything. Man's ego, man's sexual desires, man's words, man's ability to love and even man's desire for God must change to within oneself not from outside their self.

No angel ever came here to say how great everything is. It is not their mission, many were thrown out of the higher realms for one major reason, that was their own ego. Animals have a soul. They can come back as a human in some cases. Few can stay in the astral world depending on their owner in their last life.

Crystals have a different form of life. They are energy holders. On Easter Island, they found many skeletons with a hole cut in the top of their heads. It was so they could remove the crystals that were inside the human brain for the knowledge they learned. They were all in sitting position. The most significant difference between plants and humans is awareness. Humans can change theirs. A grain of sand stays that for a very time.

A medicine woman I studied with taught about speaking to trees, rocks and meeting the earth spirits. They watched and witnessed history. They could not do a thing about it except leave like they are doing now. Trees help you ground to the earth. The elementals are all living beings. They are fun to be with but they are disappearing too.

She taught about all the elementals. I met most of them. They are all leaving this world just because of man.

Mermaids and the other mythical creatures that were here at one time or another are leaving or did. They have no place to stay here.

On the topic of Bigfoot, Native people speak about them as good. They have never done anything good for humans. I have a friend, who claimed that he was working with them for 40 years. I had him and his wife, as guests on my radio show. I told him I would debate him. He said ok. When I did after 1.5 hours he was so upset. I said it was over. People that deal in dream land cannot face any truth.

Because you studied Marshal arts all your life doesn't mean anything other than you might be good at it. It doesn't make you a better person even though most think it does.

I was going to be a boxer when I was young. I met my first wife. She was worried about me so I switched to Aikido. I became a brown belt. Before I switched to another style, I decided my spiritual quest was much more important.

Killing is not forgivable. When I was with Jesus He did explain that, not that many people listened. It is in the Bible and yes, a few things are important for people if you can find them.

What do you really believe? You might say you are spiritual not me. No one is spiritual if they don't know GOD.

People like the Dali Lama, Deepak Chopra, the Pope, Eckhart Tolle and all the other people have an incredible following bigger than Jesus ever did. Does that make them spiritual or more important? I can say no from the core of my heart. I can only compare them to when Jesus was alive.

People follow Jesus now without knowing anything about Him other then what they read. How many people know anything about what He really did or who He really was? What people read in the Bible has little truth about Him. He was so much more.

What do you think is important? It is who you listen to and allow to fill your conciseness with. Who do you respect, worship and study with? There is no connection to God no matter what that is.

Please don't hate me for saying that. If
you agree you might think you are a fool.

Things of this world must be let go
including the idea that you are important.
Most people cannot or will not go there.
It is so hard for two people to just get
along never mind the entire world. Having
children and pets takes a giant toll on your
own growth.

Why be one with your work? Is it
helping humans in any way really? You
cannot say giving a sad or angry person a
drink is helping. It is always easier to hide
from the truth then dealing with it.

Is there a perfect family? Really? Man
has created a picture of what is right and
most people except it. Why? The brain has
very little space for spiritual awareness.
Ideas created out of the programmed
brain, with no spiritual truth will never
help mankind move forward spiritually. It
cannot, and will not.

Jesus taught about leaving the body and it will take you many places. He never meant for people to stay here. Why do Christians think He will come back and take them? He did not the first time, did He? Only a few souls left with Jesus.

I can tell you this in Jesus' own words "there will be many greater than He", do people listen? A person must be brain dead that cannot understand what He is saying? Are you such a fool to think anything can be greater than God? Jesus never said He was that. I was there, were you? So why make Him a God?

Living with Jesus for a brief time allowed me to learn more than what I could in hundred lifetimes or even more. He was the only soul I know that radiated light over everything and everyone He walked near. When He was being tortured Yes, His light started dying in the physical body. They were making sure of that.

Why did I come back to this world after being with Jesus? It took me most of my life to understand that myself. It was not to save the world.  It was about understanding Love. God's love not man's. It was man that tried to destroy everything about it when they killed Jesus. That is the image from the physical world, after many death experiences and seeing my past lives, seeing that soul-after death can move much further in Its awareness and what it can really do there.

What is Jesus doing now, why would He come back? Because man's ego is thinking they are important to GOD?

Foolish people think they are important. Inside themselves they know that is not true. They will get programmed to believe that. A few famous singers and artists give back to this world. Many skills, jobs and professions give nothing back to spirit at all. How many souls have any truth to bring out?

You will find out when you die, if you are truly as aware as you think you are. If you are aware of what is really happening at that time. If not, you will never know who you are, right at that moment or ever. You will be starting over here again. Don't worry you have a chance to learn something again.

Are you still debating if there really is life after death? No matter what your experiences are telling you, you are still alive in a physical body. Living within its program ideas. That is what I call Hell.

If you had a death experience, you have a starting point of understanding soul. Something someone else cannot teach you. There are out-of-body experiences that can help you as well. When Jesus was teaching, He explained what to look for and how to know you are protected. He also taught what things not to do, and there are plenty.

The first important being not to tell spirit where you need to go. Don't ever try to tell God what to do, ever.

Ego and self-worth, thinking what you deserve and what you don't, will end the experience instantly. Don't expect a certain angel or guide. Don't expect one of your family members either. You must be open. The guides appointed to you are right for you whether you agree or not.

You cannot have truth if you did not experience it. That starts in the physical with the acceptance of aliens and things like Bigfoot, lost souls and entities.

I know many people except things just from hearing about it. Many individuals accept pictures as proof regardless of who took them. They accept anything that feels good. I hear the top UFO people calling one of the top magicians an advanced alien.

Stage magic stayed around because of man's desire for supernatural things to be real, then believing in it. Have you ever wondered why in the old days aliens, angels and entities ran around on planet earth? Years later more people excepted nature spirits instead. Today we have many more people that have no awareness about the psychic, astral or dimensional worlds or realms. It's not hard to understand why Jesus will not incarnate back.

When He was alive He spoke about people being greater than He was. That has not happened and to tell the truth men are becoming the opposite, leading people further and further away from the truth and God Itself. They fill up with ego making them feel great about themselves, making themselves better than everyone else. I repeat this because it is a very important idea for thinking if Jesus will come back.

All things are affected by all the conditions around it. That meaning many

things change just by the time and place
of it happening. People think they are
important in the idea that they can
destroy the earth. They cannot make it
better.

People try so hard to follow their
dreams without any idea where they really
come from. I will never say follow a
religion. They have lost anything
important within it. Man's idea of what is
better is deteriorating.


Here are what (spiritual people say)


"All that we are is the result of what we
have thought, with our thoughts, we make
the world." – Gautama Buddha
That would mean a world of sick deviates,
sick abusive and homeless people and yes,
it is filled with that.

"Let yourself be silently drawn by the strange pull of what you really love. It will not lead you astray." – Rumi

Guess he thought people's idea of what is important was important. No matter how perverted or twisted they are.

I guess all the killings in the name of Love is OK for most people.

Experiences

I am going back to speak about experience. People searching for an enjoyable experience, what do you think people experienced when Jesus was alive? What would be good in those days? It is not hard to think of what most people would call a valuable or enjoyable experience.

That is a main idea I need to get you to understand over everything else. Good is a programed idea. Does good help one

grow and if it does how? Does it have
anything to do with understanding God? I
am not speaking about ego for it loves the
word good or feeling good. When you
compare something to something else it is
incredibly hard to say which one is better
when you already think both are good. I
call that the good the better the best idea
and nothing being wrong.

You need an experience yourself, to
know the truth. How do you decide if your
experience is real or not? Are you willing
to test it and prove it?
Ask yourself these questions:
#1 what were you doing?
#2, where were you?
#3 what was on your mind?
#4 are any drugs, drinking smoking,
partying, having sex involved?
#5 is there unquestionable evidence?
#6 was it spiritual or physical? Do you
know the difference?

#7 did you learn something to help you in your life? Outside ego.

#8 do you need to spread the word to the world about it now. Then will you?

I don't care what people say about experiences. You can have them to learn. Can you explain it to someone else, really? Most truths are for all souls that are aware not just one. It is if you are on a journey home. It does not change ever. That journey will never end.

I had many experiences in my life that blew me away. Many I never went into with any one. Some I was more than willing to speak about. Many people are afraid to speak about their experiences because of losing it. I am not but do not want everyone trying to have the same one.

There are two sides of the truth. Where ever you walk leave no footprints or leave a trail for someone to follow. Each has a different meaning to the one that had the experience. Many were told not to give away their secrets. No one can go past the little Gods or deities with what someone else told them.

When you get older in life many things change, like how much of what you thought was real becomes, was it important? Is there something after death? You can say you believe as many things as you want but as death sneaks in everything you know or don't know will be in your face.

I faced death many times. One time as I was drowning I saw my whole life in that time, and a few others as well. I was still inhaling water breathing underwater in that. I am not sure how. Spirit said life or death is my choice. After I saw my life I said give me just a little bit more time to finish one more book. Which I am finishing now. Years later after so many attacks on this book. It is coming out to you.

I was shown what I came here for. I did have another death experience after that. It was so different. In a total of five they were all different. One experience is just that. One truth is only one as well. Hopefully each leads you to the next that you need to take. One will not give you all the answers you want. Saying that it will, is again another lie. There is only one important truth when you are done when you finally find it. A true God.

Many people will ask you, when you are speaking about God, are you speaking about the Puppet master pulling the strings? Many people believe that. They will never truly understand any kind of a real God. That is why many people now think they are God. Not one person can prove it in any way. Ego is in full control on those who think they are.

Please listen to everything I say before you try to make up your own truth about it all.

People like Rev. Faricon are speaking about ships (UFO'S). No religion has a clue to any alien agenda. Even though they incorporated it. Many are trying to say Jesus was an alien.

It's not like they have any proof of aliens really helping man become spiritual or aware of God. They did know how to kill.

The Hindu people of India followed many deities. The Mayans followed many deities as well as man-made idols and created ideas about God. It allowed them to become mass killers in the name of God. The same as other religions do today. The facts that men were killing woman and children in sacrifice in many paths show where man was spiritually.

It seems all through our present history anyone showing any psychic power was called a demon and always under attack and killed. If Jesus were to come back today, what do you think people of all the different religions would do to deal with that? Would He not be called a danger to the world? Ignorant people living in a program think it could come out good for who, them? The people thinking, they would be saved? How about the way it went down the first time, wouldn't it be the same? How many life times must go by before man decides to find the truth? The truth that was always right in front of their face. Jesus made sure of that. People calling everything He did a fake are still here.

What humans do with their own people in the name of their own religion is sick. The six basic religions which are the main reason for all the wars we had and have now.

Let's talk about stories

Not just in the Native Nations but all Nations that told many stories to entertain their children. The greater the story the more it was accepted.

I'm not sure how you can draw a line from facts to fiction. I would start with using common sense. Then just look at the real world. It is something you should do with everything you hear no matter who says it, including me.

I am not going to mention all the big names in the UFO world and New Age world telling the stories they tell. The fairy tales and the programmed ideas and all the false info leading people into acceptance of aliens as saviors and being one with God. The entire world is going to be spiritual soon.

There were a few around always, telling man, he is God. I would not have the money to fight them all in court but I would win every case in truth. How much can a person charge for their service? That would depend on the size of their ego and the amount of programming they had.

Jesus spoke about the people that other people will follow. The number of false prophets that will be here. How demons and spirts will cause serious problems to the way we live. How not to get trapped by the entities that think they have the truth.

Some angels will be able to guide you to the next level you will take. How to keep oneself protected always, from anything psychic attacking you. That is something very few people know or even believe, while they are under the spell, course or programming from them. He spoke about races coming here with their own agendas, which all alien races have.

Still all this does not help one find their true self, understand their Soul or anything even closely relating to what God is. You must know everything about God to understand IT.

Today I see the number one problem on learning is we have few teachers able to teach anything important. All the things learned in school, how many times will the normal, average person use any of it? Most of his-story is lies. English is about man made words that are accepted. Words man thinks we can all understand.

Many are accepted and are not truly understood at any level.

Back to the people destroying this world, making lots of money. People want to believe something good is happening. People now think good aliens are going to help. That we are all connected to God. (even if that were true) we would have to be aware of what we are connected to. That meaning an understanding of GOD. If that is not true the rest is not true.

Understanding that has nothing to do with the ideas man created over thousands of years ago of what God should be. The way man thinks what God's traits are. Are God's traits loving, giving, caring, compassionate? Those traits do not relate to anything about God in our world. They are only words of a lost soul looking for redemption of one's own ego. People are hiding from their own actions. It is the reason man created the idea of Hell being somewhere else other than earth. That again is so wrong.

If there was a giant bon fire and a few people were throwing children into the fire, where does Hell exist? You can say in a person's mind, yes but it exists here not on another dimension. Soul's minds are bad here. Let go of the idea we are all part of God. Earth has all the hell beings of the universe, starting with the root race of their tribes here.

I will not go back into Atlantis. Man will never except the truth about it, even when they find it.

The people building the pyramids had ideas about coming back to the body they had before they died. Why? Whatever little gods they were following taught them. In experiences, they were shown how that would happen, causing them to believe that. Coming back to a sick old dead body, again why? I cannot perceive anything important from that idea, except a person so attached to earth they just don't want to leave it. They hold on to anything they think will keep them here.

They were never given any more than an idea about soul reincarnating. If man was going to be your slave forever you would not want them to be smart enough to leave, would you? The same as Lucifer has domain over many people that live here. God allows it not Lucifer.
That is the biggest answer to life and death, being able to understand it from a spiritual view point, not a giant ego. One that is growing bigger every day. It is here on earth. Lucifer is not creating all the pain and suffering, man is. Lucifer just feeds the fire.

We have dimensional beings saying much of nothing to everyone, just like the so called spiritual people. They have no knowledge but remarkable stories. It pulls them into the dream world like many want you to live in. Some of the futurist say, "living the dream" yes, in dreamland. What would be important about watching a bird fly, or how about really flying?

I would like to say that John Lennon was spiritual. He was an aware person who was killed in December 1980. A psychic (who was John's good friend) said he was abducted by an alien race. John said he saw a ship twice in NYC. He was given an actual artifact, which he gave to Uri Gella the month before he was killed. He was one of the few people at that time, a real person, able to bring a new change to the world. The Government knew that and had to have him killed. No power wants peace. It would destroy their power.

All the speakers and religious people telling remarkable stories but did they make anything important happen? I will skip the names of the most respected people given credit for speaking about peace and love and still nothing came out of their stories. We have never been so close to world war three.

I will admit Gandhi did create a profound change. How many had to die including him for the change on earth?

Change usually means one thing. The death of lots of people. People like Noah, Lot, Gandhi, the races of certain people of Atlantis and the other civilizations all died alone that way. Few make it to see the fruits of their labor (if any)? I said before we need to leave something even our footprints.

Prayer and Enlightened people. Really?

Prayer / Enlightenment

Let's get this straight. If you are looking for what you want to hear - you are listening to the wrong person. I promise what I have been speaking about is the truth and it might not agree with your programming.

Let's get this straight good people pray and so do bad people so who's truth comes true? Do they both get their answers? Bad people get out of jail even being killers and rapists. If you think that was their prayer?

I just received a link from a (Healer) she only charges thirty- thousand dollars for her healing work. It is three months. You get to be with her for two hours then get to speak on the phone a few more hours a day over the next two months. Oh, she has a great discount today.

In my whole life, I never charged anyone I worked with. I cannot. It is against all my spiritual teaching. Yes, it is ok if someone wants to gift me that is great. On that, there is no definition of what that should be, if anything. Then swap trades is also acceptable if you need to.

In prayer, who do you really pray to? Do you pray to your created idea of whatever you believe, whether a deity, demon, alien or animal? Let's just mix them all together.

We have so many ideas about Gods, like the sun God, moon God, the water God, the earth Goddess, how about the self-God?

Let's go deeper, one with God. What does that even mean? One needs to become aware of God but not to become IT.

Jesus never claimed that He was a spiritually enlightened being.

People do think that they are God in their own mind. Really? Who gives them that power? What does an enlightened being do? Absolutely nothing on this planet. Except program other people. The idea of saving one person while a hundred die. They tell you how you should live and what you should do. They expect you to bow down at their feet. They ask you for your money. How and why do people follow that?

Man is always looking for forgiveness of not living up to his purest potential. If that was not true they would not bow down to anyone else. Man, is always looking for someone else's truth. While they sit there saying they have the truth. Never thinking about what Jesus really brought to this world. They will follow anyone else's truth.

Fully Enlightened means what?
For most people, their ego thinks it knows something. My idea of what it should mean is it has a power, super psychic powers and abilities that others don't know.

Tell me right now one person that really does have any abilities that a God has, and can prove it? Try raising a mountain, raise the dead, or anything incredible as Jesus did. I am sure they can tell an exceptional story. They can hypnotize people to except a view point.

They want people to see their programmed vision. People like stories and want them to become real. If the Ten Commandments were each put into a cool story people might have excepted them.

New age people are taking people on a programed (psychic) trip making them think that whatever they want is real and important.

I mentioned, if you look in one's eyes and see an ocean of blue light. You feel it fill your whole being. You are standing in front of a person going through purification.

We are in the twenty-first century many things changed in the past ten years alone. Religions, spiritualism, and demonism as paths all leading people astray from the truth. Then you have your good old father and mother's truth with their programmed truth and ideas. Locked in the dogma of all their past lives.

The Bible talks about man being in ITs image. Man made that image. How many people on the planet except God or think of it as a person?

There are many books written about the Gods of ancient times. There are many new translations of what someone's old story is. If they had it for them self they never let it out mainstream. It has become worse over the past century.

The New Agers will say their stories are real. They will say the Bible is not real and neither is the story of Jesus. They believe many other speakers and religionist's stories. Are any of the others true? I say no. If any were, why is the world filled with people, still so sick and slowly destroying themselves? Losing all morals living in the passions instead of the truths. This will bring the downfall of humanity.

It's even more dangerous when a person starts clamming enlightenment for what are they doing. What abilities are they using? It usually means nothing. They are remarkable storytellers.

Are you ready to open your thinking? Can you imagine (again) becoming a drop of water in the ocean. What are you the ocean or the drop of water. That answer Is simple. You are part of the ocean. Does that make you feel better? Does that make you more powerful? Well as a drop of water you are not, but as an ocean you are. Water can turn to steam and rise as well. It can be frozen back into a block of ice. Soul is not a drop of water.

Each world after the astral plane becomes more incredible. Being able to live and function without pain, without seeing suffering, without dealing with lying and cheating. No killing or thinking about it. No sex as we know it.

The movie Barbarella came out with a future idea about sex many years ago. Very interesting idea at that time. They are the worlds Jesus taught about getting to.

The part that I think scares many men, who start becoming aware, is the idea of giving up sex as they know it.

Why is it all new age speakers only speak about things that make people believe all things are good?

Like all magnets, things influence each other in this world. The closer you get the more it affects. The closer together the more it effects everyone. A stronger magnet pulls them all to it.

Jesus gave man the only way out. Not through drugs, ego or money, it was through soul awareness.

For anyone who has been abducted, they no longer can understand God's truth. They are dealing with a created program and stories given to them in two ways. One by the aliens. One is the Government. How much is provable?

How many people have anything to help take them further in life except stories? There is never evidence, does anyone even see that?

Aliens and the Government have been able to keep everything at a complete deadlock and under full control. Man's desire to believe has nothing to do with God. They will usually say the good aliens created their new world experiencers.

Saving lives matter, for who? One's family? If you are speaking about the Government killing, most have such a ridiculous salary for killing, they should get paid nothing.

One hundred and sixty million dollars for one boxer fighting someone is perverted. That could help an unimaginable amount of people. Morals are completely lost. Who is spending all their money? Many family men.

I describe myself with two words Incarnate realist. It speaks for everything I say and do.

I learned at a very early age magic or psychic abilities don't really make things better. How is it people don't ever look at the truth? Taking slaves and giving them freedom to do the same thing to other people or just right out killing them.

Now I am taking a giant step here. God doesn't speak to anyone, ever. It allows a small part of IT's wisdom to be understood. Anyone saying God told them to do anything really that is not free will of soul. Which is one reason why soul is here. To learn it's truth.

Who would be able to tell us the truth other than God? If God allowed us to see IT?

The stories are just that - aliens playing with our DNA. Who is playing with theirs? If that story was even true. Man is making it true.

Jesus did not teach about aliens even though He knew they were there. They only can slow us down on reaching true awareness or spiritual truth.

How could the story of Adam and Eve have even been proven to anyone? That whole story is a programmed idea. I say it was created by a reptilian race. It uses the plural of Gods and makes God a liar within it.

So, the whole story about Adam and Eve is a lie.

Most people want to blame every other religion or path for the problems rather than looking at themselves.

The trouble starts with aliens, demons or even a sick Government. They all can step in because people don't know what protection means. Even if it means death of the body. For the people with eyes and ears, the promise land does not exist on this planet. It never did.

If one prays to God and God tells you to kill someone you really need to think about what kind of a God you are really dealing with.

Something I think is very sick is when a so-called high spiritual enlightened person thinks they are beyond ego, lies and the programs of the body. They then tell other people their stories and want them to believe their own truth. It might be very important to them. When in history did it ever really help? If it did WHO? Think about that.

There are only a few exceptions to that rule ever. Saul (Lot) was told about Sodom and Gomorra before it happened and even science admits it happened not the same way it says in the Bible.

Noah was told and followed through with what he was told and saved many creatures on part of the planet.

If you believe in evolution you don't need to pray for you will evolve into something no matter what you do.

Man coming from ape and ape coming from an ameba is ridiculous. God decides when anything really changes. Many of the craziest ones were all destroyed. God decided something greater needed to be here. God uses what IT created to affect the things that are here.

Science makes it sound accidental. If one thing changes it would take millions of other things to happen in super extended time. That meaning to create even the heart of a person by accidents would take billions of years, if it came from a grain of dust from a meteorite. (impossible).

Why did the mythical beings that were here leave, ever wonder why that happened? Do you think science can ever speak about all the different earth spirits?

When man was created he was a spiritual being like they all were. After Atlantis was destroyed by alien races that abused them and turned them into killers. Atlantis had to be destroyed. What was left became the four races that are here now. They are all mass killers praying to a false god. If there were none they would create one.

At that point why would you need to pray? The Mayan race were always mass killers so how do any people call them a spiritual race? They prayed to a false God.

I will tell you the truth. You can listen or not. The true God allows anyone searching for IT and deserves It, to find It's truth. The little gods do not. They give you a false truth to follow.

Now let's speak about Enlightenment.

It is a little different depending on what path you follow. How did Jesus describe it? Enlightenment deals with understanding one's mind. One learns that you are soul not the mind.

Why do all people link spiritual with enlightenment?  Why do they accept teachings by certain people?

They are supposed to be better than most. Some people say they are aliens. Are they really of this plane? If you check most paths you will find their root-foundation will bring in aliens and coming from space. It is even in Buddhism.

What do you think and what do you think you know? What is a reason for IT, meaning God and what is the reason for Soul?

Where do aliens fit in? They are all creating a false belief, a false truth for people to follow. All lies to hold them to this world.

Their words repeat each other's words. Not one has an original idea unless they claim an alien was with them and Jesus together being on a space ship.

The Governments falling apart are trying to create fear but they are creating even more problems They try to make everyone work together. Our own Government is afraid of the truth coming out so they add false truth. Peoples truth about Spiritual growth, that we are all one group consciences, is the biggest lie to mankind. When it should be individual to each soul. You can always believe what you want. I went over that already.

Another controlling idea is why humans were brought here.

Why Jesus was the only one to bring out the truth, would be the reason why he was killed.

Jesus was one of the few beings in our world that had real communication with GOD. He did not deal with aliens. He dealt with Lucifer. I don't know anyone else that has done that and was able to speak about it.

Have you ever wondered why the miracles and events are not happening like in the Bible or any other story of the Gods? Man doesn't deserve it now. Not even the protection from earthly things. They walked away from what Jesus confirmed to them and still they did not understand.

Healing a person without giving them the teaching Jesus brought is giving a starving person an empty cup.

If one person could use all the psychic abilities or even one at one-hundred percent they would be considered a God by man.

Aliens are no better. They are only working with a small level of the world's people. I cannot tell you how much they are really doing to the planet. I can assure you everything from Chemtrails to

Fracking is all a part of it. There are reasons why any Government would allow it unless completely controlled by a higher sicker force.

Jesus said there will be every evil walking the world declaring that they are God and will bring the darkness over us all.

Jesus did not teach a religion. Aliens did. Demi Gods are the ones playing with people like a board game. Just like in the movies Jason and the Argonauts or Hercules. There are Many other remarkable stories of people with power. We have many fakers today. Saying they are all that.

Jesus gave people a new way to think and allowed them to create their truth. None of that was put in in the Bible. Only two religions I know really have a clue to a part of Jesus' teachings. Out of two-thousand religions here now, Only, three have the biggest following, which doesn't make them right either. They are all not right or even close to the truth.

Before I go further - Truth doesn't change, only the view of it does. If it does it wasn't true to begin with. It meaning you are following more lies.

Anyone telling you what you should do or how you should be are not spiritual teachers. People are not spiritual. They should only lead you to a way for you to find what you truly are looking for.

Aliens created the false dream that man holds on to of love and peace. Even though it has not been part of our planet for three or four thousand years.

They are only of the physical world thinking. It comes from within your body.

I am telling you straight from my heart after studying with many different masters, shamans, medicine people, angels, deities, out of all of them the most important truth came from Jesus alone.

If you are reading this, can you understand few people look to Jesus as a real person. You are ready to be the best you can here. Let them look to science and aliens for their truth. Even more scary they are looking to Alien knowledge to help save the world.

People speak about God being here and now. Do you think God would want to come here? IT will never come into Hell. Only IT's angels must. The demons can as well. Both are here for you to follow. You decide everyday - who you will listen to by every action, even if it is you just saying, "G** damn it."

DO people think they really can tell God what to do? Why do people really think an angels job is telling you to love everyone?

Only a few souls ever try telling God what to do and lived through it. Not because of their ego either. I don't see men ever understand that.

Everyone is looking to find spiritual power. They are looking for Money, both are not the key or the answer. They both only offer self and world destruction.

Hard truth

If you have love on this planet. Love is temporary even if it lasts two or three life times. It will end. The love that you think you have. It will be replaced by another love. There are two kinds of love for humans. They are the love of humans and the love of God. They are the two things that will grow from one slowly into the other. Many lifetimes will pass before it happens for most people. God-realization is the only true path and is the hardest. Jesus had a challenging time, telling His followers that.

If it is love of God it will always be growing. First you do need to know what God is to love it. That is Jesus' main teaching about God. How do you love IT? Sitting on the floor for hours, hiding in a cave for months or years, jumping up and down thousands of times, chanting I love you a billion times doesn't make it real.

I cry when I think about people that think earth's people are so important and need to save them. Like a chick breaking out of it shell. Save the shell really, for what?

There are a few reasons why God allows everything. Once a soul knows it cannot be killed it doesn't have to follow the rules of man and truly can start following God's words again, not man's rules. They are now able to know the difference.

Another false idea of man is no soul can be created or destroyed. They just keep changing. Whoever proved that to us? Science sure does try.

The first crucial step is seeing soul for what it really is.

When you finally open your eyes, what do you think you will see?  What were all your stories and dreams about? Do you feel they are worth the time you gave them? Are you now ready to take the next step? Jesus walked right into it freely.

When Jesus was alive here man had very few happy times. People were just trying to survive. It was a proper time and place to implant truth. If all men were only ready for it. The population was different. Woman were not equal at any level.

When Jesus came to people's homes they all opened their doors. They did not ask what His religion was. They did not have to speak about love. People suddenly felt something they never felt before. The Bible doesn't talk about the man called Jesus. They don't speak about what people really felt just by being near Him. When He did His miracles how it affected people was crazy.

How many people today, the one's that say they are one with God, can they do anything to prove it? They cannot even speak about IT meaning God.

The people speak about Jesus like reading a book. How would your friends describe you right now? How much do any one of them know about the real you?

The things you can create are not what you think. People don't walk around saying they want to create Karma. I wonder why not. I am sure the world would change instantly if they knew how much they were creating.

Jesus is alive and well.  He dwells in the higher realms. He was a master teacher.

Christianity is the highest populated religion on this planet. Does that mean anything? It would if they all knew Jesus' true teaching and not man's programed ideas of what that was.

With people like the Pope, who leads the catholic religion? Let's just mention what he is doing now. In the past two years, he said Adam and Eve is not a real story. Who is he to make that statement? He also said Hell is not real. Really, why are we living there? Heaven is not here. He rewrote two of the Ten Commandments. How can he do that? He is the Pope, the ruler. Then he said aliens are our brothers. He will teach them his religion. Just as they made the Native people become Christians or die. He hired hundreds of people to do exorcisms.

Does the Pope understand his own religion? Did he ever speak to God or Jesus? I can tell you from the core of my being he might as well create his own religion. Nothing he is doing relates to what Jesus was teaching.

Do many people know why they keep Jesus on the cross? They keep trying to feed Jesus their sins. They think He will forgive them. Then, they created confession. Do you really think any Priest on this planet has that kind of power to do that? You can live in dreamland if you believe in it.

The new age speakers are saying they are fifth or sixth dimensional beings. Does anyone out there know what that really means? Can you prove it?
Healers are saying they can cure your karma. No one can do that except yourself and God. God doesn't do it very often. If It ever does. Jesus was one of the few souls on this planet able to do that, meaning you will go to a higher realm not just the astral plane. Every healer right now thinks they can give you your energy back meaning making you think you are healed. It is only temporary, because you still have your karma to deal with sooner or later.

Mohammad met with Gabriel two times. The first time he did not know who it was.

I wonder why? Funny the second time he knows. How's that? Did the angel say I am Gabriel? Then he believed it? How many people today say they are working with three of the highest angels in the Bible. Don't forget the angels fell from grace. That means the higher realm.

If an angle came up to you how would you know who it is unless they tell you and you believe them. Right? It is not like they have three lion heads, then again you would need to except someone's story about it.

Final


If you ever read the Bible, I must say I did many times. Every major event was preceded by an angel.

If you get anything out of all I said please try to understand you are the center of your universe and live in a body here so you live in both. You have the responsibility to learn how to work in both and prepare for when you leave the physical. You will do it alone. If you cannot get past that you will never get into the higher worlds. You will dwell in the physical and astral worlds forever. You will never experience the incredible worlds beyond all the things you are programmed to believe.

Lust, love, anger, hate, compassion, desire, feelings, pain, suffering all need to be let go of if you have any real desire to know a real God. Yes, even your relationships will disappear if you want to reach the highest realm. I never spoke about a man-made God as being anything right or important. No one had ten percent of His abilities. He gave up His body to show the world the truth.

Soul is always growing no matter how slowly it seems. When soul becomes aware it just might not want to move any higher but surly not backwards.

The idea of oneness, ok but that is one with yourself and God now. You are creating where you will be at any given time in the higher realms. Now enjoy what you have been working so hard to get to.

You are not God. But you are now one with it. That means living within GOD's truth. You become a co-creator of your own worlds while you are in IT's.

Peace, happiness and love on your journey. Remember every step you will take gets harder to take but greater the rewards in every way. The greater you become, the more like God you now are becoming. That has nothing to do with this world or the stuff going on here. There is always a reason for spiritual growth which never has anything to do with the lower realms.

God created a place for soul to start its mission and very few people will ever learn that truth. So please take everything I said as the truth or as close to God truth as I can say. Compare it to any other teaching for no one ever speaks about a real God. Jesus was the most important person to do that and not any master because most say they are that and working with It.

After sixty-five years of experience. I remember most of it. I do not understand why people are so far off track as to why they really are here. I hear it is the vices of the people that make it great.

With all the twisted lies and all the misinformation, they pick to follow the greatest deceivers. The false teachers, the exceptional story tellers and even the evilest religious leader.

If that is not bad enough, to follow a sick Government, not that any is good around the world. I am sure there a few small countries doing good.

Now more than ever in all our history has there been so much proof of aliens and UFO's and still no one speaks about it in a tangible way. They treat it the same as they treat Jesus creating a story they like. Making it sound like a good thing.

That leaves people to pray to man-made ideas about what God is. That program you to believe earth is important. If that was close why would aliens be abducting and eating people?

Sure, you can hide in your box and let this world keep you locked to the idea this is where souls need to be.

In a year or so they will see the abilities aliens have. They are trying to duplicate. I am not sure why. It will never help man understand God. Every religion speaks about God as what they want It to be. Rather than what It really is.

Jesus is not what man wants Him to be either. If you kill someone, He will not be the one forgiving you. Guess why? He cannot. It is one of the spiritual laws and they can never be compromised.

Please take everything I said to heart. I did not intend to make money on this book. I will give my life to promote it and the truth within it. If I was wrong about anything you will see it in the world.

Love is the root to all evil, well at least man's idea of what it is. When people give a one-hundred percent to love, then they will know what it is. Know you might never get any of it back.

In Love and light   Last final thought.

If you are a parent you really need to think about what you teach your child. What you will leave them in this world they must stay in. But even more important, what will they have when they leave this world? Jesus left that truth but one must find it. There are no second chances. Reincarnation is not a second chance. It is the last chance. You cannot compare the physical body to the astral body or the mental body to the soul body. They each deal differently with what they can do and what they are. What soul thinks changes so do the experiences from the physical world. They do not help the soul body but how many people will ever try to get to that level. If they are listening to aliens they will never leave the lower worlds. Don't accepts the imperfections of the human mind as it has many and that is very important to understand.

May you search out truth about God.


In Truth only    Tommy Hawksblood



List of definition.



*A1. Aliens, we are all aliens from some other place. We did not get created on earth. There are aliens playing with us as puppets. Many souls are weak and open to it. That includes killing. Aliens and demons are not the same but what they do is similar in some ways. Most races need one thing. The same thing that everyone here needs. (food). It sure is not spiritual awareness like so many people believe.

*A2. Angels, are bringers of warnings. They do lead people through the doorway (light) to the astral world. They are not the teachers.

*A3. Ascending, when soul lets go of the physical body and moves into the Astral world. All people do it when they die unless they become a lost soul and stay here as a Ghost or spirit.

*A4. Ascension, something many people say they go through or did. It is only for a few souls in the history of the planet.

Jesus was the only one I know that went through it, then proved it.


*A5. Astral Body, is the second body soul moves into after it leaves the physical body. It is not the same by any means. It takes on an age usually twenty-five to thirty-five on the astral plane. There's no need for babies there. That has a lot to do with crib death. The Astral body now has the same soul as when you were here. The difference is the astral body doesn't have the physical parts a human body had, like the heart or brain. It also doesn't have a nervous system like we do here. It cannot be killed by anything other than God. All people think every soul will live forever. A complete lie. If God cannot reform a soul even after a thousand times of reincarnating, the soul is still evil it can be destroyed. It will become energy that will not have an awareness. Gods greatest gift to soul.


*b1. Bliss state, it is a state of being void of everything including awareness, standing/floating in the light and sound on the top of the astral plane. Nothing matters or is important. There is light and the sound in that state. It can be timeless or it can be passed through, that is your choice.

*b2. Box, An idea of living in a small space four walls and no windows, a floor and a top with no windows, no doors. You were told it is heaven and believe it. You know nothing other than the box. You are told to be happy and you think you are.

*D1. Deity, a being on one of the other realms, that have power over anything below it. There are Deities that are Gods each of a certain realm. All the lower worlds have one main one except the astral world.

   a. God deities. Are the ones that control the whole realm they dwell on. Every soul going into the next realm must past each one. There is something that must happen for that to be allowed.


*G1. Guides, are the beings that have something to teach to certain people that are ready for moving forward in their true spiritual path.

*H1. Hell, what man did to earth after destroying it or allowed it to get destroyed by other beings saying they were Gods. Where killing and abuse lives now.

*I2. IT, meaning God. God being the true creator of all life in all worlds and realms. IT is not male or Female. It is not what people think IT is by no means. IT is not the programmed idea of love and light, all caring loving being.

*I3. Incarnitiate, A person that is aware of all their lifetimes and came back to finish all things in the lower world most will not come back again when they finish out that life.

*I4. Incarnation, means coming back into the physical body after you become aware of being on the astral plane of all your past lives that you lived before. It will usually be the last time you will come back.

*K1 Killing taking someone else's life. Taking away one's body from soul.

Crucifixion, put on a cross to die. Usually nails through one's wrists and ankles. Jesus was an being tortured for days first then even stabbed while on the cross. Then feed vinegar to him to drink.

*L1. The Light, is what radiates out of God ITSELF. It comes down through all the higher worlds into the lower realms. All the way to the physical world. It is part of what connects us to IT and sustains soul's life. The light keeps getting brighter as you get closer and closer to God. It only takes on three colors white yellow and blue. Blue being in the lower words. They say white is only a shading in the physical world, it is what God radiates as. Blackness does not exist in many places in the higher realms or if it does can be filled with anything a higher soul wants there.

*L2. Lucifer, a fallen angel, allowed to do what he does from the astral plane to the physical. He excepts his followers and God allows it to. When one does follow him, they are now trapped in earths hell. That means ones twisted ideas of fun.

*M1. Mary M, short for Mary Magdalene.

*R1. Realist, taking one's experience from life and living within in that. The truth that you except as real.

*R2. Reincarnation, something that most souls do over and over without awareness of their past lives. They will until they pay off most of their karma -they made in this world. Most souls have no right to say what they are going to reincarnate into unless their karma is just right. Usually it is not. There is ninety-two percent of the world suffering that did not decide to come back to an abused starving person.

*S1. Sin/karma, what you will have to work off before you get to leave earth permanently.  There are a few things that will give you many lifetimes to work off if committed.

*S2. Soul body, the last body. It is not male or female. It is pure light. It has total awareness of Itself as it does of God now. It became a reflection of Gods laws. Soul now, can do two things. One stay there or move out of the soul body into the next higher realm.

*S3. The Sound, radiates out of God from the highest realm to the lowest but as it does it changes vibration itself. Each realm, it is in is different. It is how God speaks to all things. Not in any kind of words just vibration. That vibration also changes meaning from the lower realms to the higher realms. Nothing in the higher realms relate to anything here as we know it.